Vision

An Aromatherapy Bible Study

A HOLY SCENTS™ BIBLE STUDY

WENDY SELVIG

&

YVONNE PACE

Copyright © 2017 Selvig Enterprises, INC. Book design copyright © 2017 Growing Healthy Homes LLC™. All rights reserved. No part of this book may be reproduced, stored, or transmitted in any form or by any means, electronic, mechanical, photocopying or recording without the express written permission of the author and publisher with the exception of photocopying the Weekly Review pages and the final chapter for the purpose of cutting and pasting vision statements to a vision board. All Scripture references, except when noted, are NIV (New International Version).

ISBN: 978-0-9988534-4-4
Printed in the United States of America
First printing.

Growing Healthy Homes LLC
P.O. Box 3154
Bartlesville, OK 74006

To obtain additional copies of this book, please visit
www.GrowingHealthyHomes.com.

Disclaimer: The authors of this book are not physicians, nor do they want to be your physicians. The information in this book is for educational purposes only and as a guideline for your personal use. It should not be used as a substitute for medical counseling with a health care professional. It is not intended to diagnose, treat, cure, or prevent any disease or illness. If you have an illness or a medical condition, please consult the health care provider of your choice. These statements have not been evaluated by the Food and Drug Administration (FDA). These products are not intended to diagnose, treat, cure or prevent any disease.

The authors are not liable for the misuse or misunderstanding of any information contained within this publication.

Table of Contents

About the Authors 6

Acknowledgments 7

Introduction 11

Laying the Spiritual Foundation........................17

Notes for Bible Study Leaders...........................20

WEEK 1

To Perish or Succeed 25

Writing Down the Vision 31

When God Takes Up Your Cause – Global Vision.......37

Making A Local Impact 43

Week 1 Review & Meditation............................48

WEEK 2

Vision For Your Family......................................51

Vision For Your Vocation...................................57

Vision For Your Spiritual Life............................63

Vision For Your Emotional Health 73

Week 2 Review & Meditation............................83

WEEK 3

Vision For Your Health......................................87

Vision For Fun 93

Vision For Your Finances...................................99

Vision For Your Relationships 107

Week 3 Review & Meditation..........................113

WEEK 4

Who Am I – Part 1...117

Who Am I – Part 2...121

30 Days From Now 125

Week 4 Review & Meditation..........................128

Assembling Your Vision Board 131

About the Authors

Wendy Selvig is a Certified Aromatherapist, and she has a degree in Bible from Manhattan Christian College and a degree in Music Composition & Technology from Oral Roberts University. She is a paid natural health researcher for a non-profit organization, as well as a published author and independent distributor for Young Living Essential Oils. Her love for natural health and for God and His Word are perfectly married in this Aromatherapy Bible Study series!

Yvonne Pace has been a practicing Physical Therapist for more than 30 years. Yvonne combines her knowledge of physical therapy with almost a decade of experience in using essential oils topically, aromatically and nutritionally. She is also a Young Living independent distributor. Yvonne and her husband have lived in Colorado Springs for the last 40 years, where they've raised two sons.

Acknowledgments

Thank you Jesus for being my Counselor on this project. You are my Lord, Savior, Friend, Deliverer, and Business Partner. I'd like to thank my good friend Yvonne for coming up with the idea of writing on the topic of Vision. I'm so happy she agreed to be a part of this project. I'd also like to thank our mentor, Sera Johnson, for showing us the way and for introducing us to Young Living Essential Oils. So glad she said YES to the Lord so many years ago and that He has connected us all on this journey. Last but not least, to each person who is on Team Faith Builders, thank you for being a "Faith Builder" and for living and walking the Young Living lifestyle with me. — *Wendy*

With a heart full of gratitude, thank you to those whom I have been blessed to have in my life who have been instrumental in helping me accomplish this study entitled *Vision:* My Savior, the Lord Jesus, without You I cannot accomplish any task set before me in this life; Wendy, my sister in Christ, for inviting me to join you in this adventure of writing a study on the Scriptures and the wonders of essential oils; and thank you Bob, my husband, for always encouraging me to develop my life interests, goals and accomplishments. I also want to thank my Pastors, Ted and his wife Gayle, our friends for over 25 years, with whom Bob and I have walked through the "experiences of life." Your friendship is a treasure that is not often found on this earth. — *Yvonne*

Welcome!

WHAT YOU WILL NEED FOR THIS STUDY:

You will need a bottle of essential oil that helps stimulate creativity and faith. Some recommendations are Young Living Envision™ or Frankincense.

Envision™ was formulated to stimulate internal drive and to help you overcome emotional blocks and fears. It is also designed to help you renew focus and stimulate your intuitive and creative abilities. It's perfect for creating a vision! Below is a list of the oils in this blend. We think you will see why it may be good choice for this study:

Spruce is calming, grounding, and is known to promote peace of mind. It supports a healthy bronchial system and breathing. It also supports healthy joints and nerves.

Geranium has been used for centuries for benefits to the skin. It may help to promote healthy teenage skin, keeping it cleansed and revitalized. It supports healthy replication of cells and healthy blood flow. It stimulates and supports the liver and pancreas and can also help to release negative memories and ease nervous tension. It is balancing to the emotions and fosters hope.

Orange is uplifting and calming. Because it is photosensitive, which means it can cause your skin to be more sensitive to the sun, care needs to be taken if you are out in the sun within 48 hours after applying it topically.

Lavender has multiple functions. If you're not sure which oil to use in a situation, you can count on Lavender being a good choice. Among many uses, Lavender supports a healthy respiratory system, healthy blood pressure, healthy skin, a healthy head of hair, a good night's sleep, and it supports your nerves. It is calming, relaxing, balancing and has been documented to improve concentration and mental acuity.

Sage supports healthy hormone levels in men and women. It can provide relief from menstrual discomforts, and it supports a healthy liver. It also supports the circulatory system and can be mentally stimulating. Avoid if you are epileptic or if you have high blood pressure. In these cases, consider choosing Frankincense for this study.

Rose has been used for applications to the skin for thousands of years. It supports and protects DNA, and helps cells to replicate normally. It promotes a healthy heart, and can help to bring balance and harmony to emotions during times of stress.

Frankincense is a wonderful choice for this study as well. Frankincense has been used for centuries for spiritual applications around the world. It promotes spiritual awareness and improves and uplifts the spirit. Frankincense stimulates the limbic system of the brain (the center of the emotions) and the hypothalamus, pineal and pituitary glands. There are over 50 references to Frankincense in the Bible. There are different varieties of Frankincense available. We like two: *Boswellia carteri* and *Boswellia sacra*. These varieties are known to stimulate specific areas of the brain that are also stimulated through prayer. *Boswellia sacra* (Sacred Frankincense) is a variety that has been reserved for royalty in the Mid-East for centuries. It is believed to be the species brought to baby Jesus by the Magi.

Whether you choose Envision™ or Frankincense (choose one; not both), diffusing the scent while you are meditating on God's Word, will help your brain to create associations between the scripture, the topic, and the aroma.

Board Materials: You will be creating a "vision board." You will be asked to gather your own materials for this. You can use a corkboard, a white board or even a poster board or piece of paper. We like corkboards, but this is *your* project so you get choose what materials you want to use! It can be any size you wish. A vision board is something you will be able to hang on your wall that will keep your vision before you. Habakkuk 2:2 talks about "writing down the vision, that heralds may run with it." The final goal of this study will be to complete a vision board to help you (and others) focus on your vision, and therefore help you accomplish it.

Spiral bound notebook for additional journaling. You may wish to have this for additional space for writing down your thoughts and prayers.

Introduction

Leader Notes: If you are leading this Bible Study with a group, this is the section you would introduce during your first meeting. The purpose is to make sure everyone is comfortable with how the study works and with using essential oils.

Welcome to this Holy Scents™ Aromatherapy Bible study! During the course of this study, you will be meditating on scripture, reading devotionals and journaling insights while using various aromatherapy techniques to enhance your experience.

Of all your senses, your sense of smell is the only one directly tied to the emotional center of your brain (the limbic brain). So when you smell a scent, your limbic brain forms an opinion about the smell and invokes an emotional response. You may wrinkle your nose in distaste, or raise your eyebrows in delight. You create an immediate opinion about the smell, and you experience an emotion. And what happens when you have an emotion about something? You remember it better! Thus, combining aromatherapy with meditation and study helps you to create stronger mental associations.

This study is on the topic of vision, and is designed to help you find the vision and purpose God has for your life. The Word of God says that without a vision, the people perish (Proverbs 29:18). We believe God has a purpose and a plan for you, and we want to help you find it. Getting the scriptures that pertain to this topic into your mind and heart is an important part of this process. Smelling the essential oil during your study time will stimulate your emotional brain and make stronger connections between scripture and heart.

We will also be guiding you to create your own vision board at the end of this study. Each day we will focus on a different area of life for which to develop a vision. You will be writing statements for those areas and putting them on your vision board at the end of the study. The intent of this project is to help you to focus and live out your purpose on a daily basis. This is going to be fun! Are you ready?

Please know that one person can do this study independently, in a small group, or in a larger Bible study setting. It also covers a lot of material in a short period of time. You may want to look through the topics and decide on your own if you or your group needs more time to cover these deep topics. Some people work at a faster pace than others. Allow yourself the ability to extend the length of the study and take two or more weeks to get through "one week" if needed. Work at your own pace or at a pace your study group is comfortable with. The most important thing is that you take adequate time to really figure out what your goals are for each area. Give yourself room if you need it.

Before we dive into the study, we need to cover some important things about working with essential oils for your safety and comfort.

Necessary Information About Essential Oils

Here are a few things to be aware of before using essential oils:

What Essential Oils Are

Essential oils are the volatile aromatic liquids that come from plant matter. They are not fatty oils that come from seeds. They differ in structure and function from fatty oils. They act as an immune system for the plant by protecting it from bacteria, fungus and viruses. They also serve as anti-freeze in cold weather. They travel up and down inside the plant administering healing where it is needed. Essential oils are very special substances. The leaves, stems, roots, flowers and sometimes branches are crushed and put through a steam distillation process. There are a few other processes to obtain oils (like cold-pressing for citrus oils), but the dominant method is distillation. The vapors are condensed, collected, and separated and contain hundreds of exciting constituents that make them very chemically complex. They are then bottled and used therapeutically for people and animals.

Purity is Very Important When Selecting Essential Oils

Because impure oils can cause health problems, it is imperative that you purchase only the highest quality therapeutic grade essential oils. We do not recommend buying anything from a grocery store or online generic retailer. Be wary of every company selling oils. Essential oils are more often compromised than not. Most essential oil companies are fairly new and not established enough to have their own distilleries. For this reason, many of them obtain oils from vendors in the perfume industry. The oils that are distilled from the perfume companies are often distilled on equipment made with toxic metals like aluminum. The oils can have metal toxins in them and you would never know it. The perfume industry can add synthetics or fillers to the oils to thin them out and make them less expensive. The cheaper the oil, the more likely it has been adulterated. It is estimated that 95% or more of the essential oil companies around the world use sub-standard practices in distillation, including the use of aluminum vats and the practice of adding synthetic chemicals to cheapen the cost of the oils. You want to seek out therapeutic grade essential oils that are safe for putting on, in and around your body. Know your oils. Many oils are not safe, even when the label says it is 100% pure. You are better off not using essential oils than to use adulterated ones. We have done extensive research and we choose to only use Young Living Essential Oils. This company has been established for over 22 years, has their own distilleries made out of surgical stainless steel, and they have an amazing proprietary process called "Seed to Seal", that guarantees purity. Every Young Living essential oil is put through a battery of tests (the latest number we saw at the lab was 15), and those tests are repeated three times. Young Living absolutely does not stand for adulterated oils. To find out more, visit SeedtoSeal.com. From the seed going in the ground, to the time the seal is put on the bottle, make sure your oil is pure.

How to Use Essential Oils

There are three primary ways to use essential oils: inhaling, applying topically, and ingesting. You can inhale an oil by diffusing it in a room. Or you can simply put a few drops of oil in your hands, rub them together and cup your hands over your nose and mouth. Breathe the aroma for at least a minute. The oils have very small molecules that float on the air. They travel from your nose, up your olfactory nerve and cross the blood/brain barrier and into your blood stream. To apply oils topically, you simply apply the oil directly on your skin. Be sure to use a carrier oil (a fatty oil like coconut or olive oil) if your skin is sensitive. For internal usage, make sure your oil is pure and the label on the bottle says that it is suitable for internal usage. You can put oils in empty vegetable capsules, or drop oils under your tongue for a sub-lingual absorption into your blood stream, or add oils to your water or food. *Again, be very careful what kind of oils you take internally. Quality is very important, and reading and heeding the label on your oil is important too!*

Safety Issues

Essential oils are generally regarded as safe (GRAS). They have been used for thousands of years, and our bodies tend to recognize plant molecules. Typically there are few, if any, side effects from using pure therapeutic grade essential oils. Always read and heed the directions on the label if in doubt. If you ever get essential oil in your eyes or if you feel an uncomfortable burning or cooling sensation on your skin, simply apply a fatty oil such as Young Living's V-6™ Vegetable Oil Complex blend, coconut oil or olive oil to dilute. The discomfort is caused by the tiny molecules of the essential oil moving through the layers of your skin so quickly that they are causing friction. Although it is not harmful, it can be uncomfortable. The large molecules of a fatty oil will grab on to the small essential oil molecules and slow down their rate of absorption, easing the discomfort. When it is necessary to apply a fatty oil to your eye, just add the fatty oil and then wipe it out. Don't use water, as it will only intensify the discomfort.

We are not doctors and do not want to be your doctors. Your Bible study leader is also not your doctor. Please do not take any thing we say as prescribing or suggesting that you make medical decisions on your own. These statements are not evaluated by the Food and Drug Administration and are not intended to diagnose, treat, cure, or prevent any disease. Please consult your physician before starting any health program.

Children and Health Concerns

It is important to remember that essential oils are very concentrated. *A little goes a long way.* Seriously, a drop or two is usually all that is needed. While the oils in the blend we are recommending are GRAS and non-toxic, children generally cannot be trusted to handle oils responsibly. Store them up out of the reach of small children. If you are pregnant, nursing, have epilepsy, or have any health concern, you should ask your doctor before using an essential oil. Be aware of your own conditions and ask your doctor if you are unsure. The blend we are recommending, Envision™, contains orange oil and is considered photosensitive. This means that your skin may be more sensitive to the sun in the 48-hours following application.

Laying the Spiritual Foundation

BY YVONNE PACE AND WENDY SELVIG

Before you dive into understanding vision for your life, we would like to lay down foundational ideas that will help you understand where we are coming from spiritually in this study. Thank you for taking the time to read this before you get started.

Since this is a Bible study, we make the assumption that you believe in and know God. But it's possible that you don't, and that's okay. We think however, that a relationship with God will greatly help you to understand some of the concepts we will discuss as we lead you through this study. We believe the idea of redemption is foundational to truly grasp the vision God has for your life, and so we want to explain it here for you.

The basics of redemption (from scripture) are this: mankind was separated from God in the beginning because of a choice to *walk away* from Him instead of choosing relationship *with* Him. God led mankind through many years of letting us see how broken we (as humans) were without Him. He originally created us for relationship with Him. Mankind had a system of sacrificing animals to atone for sin. So God entered that system and sent His Son Jesus to be the final sacrifice and the *end to the system* and old way of thinking. He said that if you believe in God and that He sent His Son, you can be restored to the place where He always wanted you to be, in a relationship with Him.

When you choose to follow Jesus, He becomes the One to whom you look to pattern your life after. You ask Him to be the Lord of your life and He puts His Holy Spirit in you. The Spirit is known as "the Counselor," and He guides your thoughts and is in your heart. There is more to it, but these are the basics of being a Christian and learning to love God and walk with Him.

So I greet you with the great words, grace and peace! We know the meaning of those words because Jesus Christ rescued us from this evil world we're in by offering himself as a sacrifice for our sins. God's plan is that we all experience that rescue.
Galatians 1:3-4 (MSG)

God's vision and plan for your life include you experiencing the grace and peace of God and being rescued from the fate of broken, fallen man. Do you know Jesus? There is a difference in knowing *about* Him and *knowing* Him. You can read and study all about Him without actually knowing Him. Though He was alive thousands of years ago, He is still alive today. God raised Him from the dead and He is now alive and sitting at the right hand of the Father in heaven, interceding (praying) for us (Hebrews 7:25). He has sent His Holy Spirit to live in and among us, and He speaks to us in various ways, including His Word (the Bible), our thoughts, peace in our hearts, and through circumstances. We can pray to Him and expect that He hears us and that He responds. But His grace and peace are gifts that we have to **acknowledge and accept**.

Jesus is the One who has redeemed us. John 3:16 tells us that "God so loved the world, that He gave His only Son. That whoever would **believe in Him**, would not perish, but have eternal life." Your belief in Him qualifies you to be "in Him." And when you are "in Him," God sees the covenant He made with Jesus when He looks at you, and you are made righteous, (which means that you are seen as you should have been, before the Fall of man). You don't gain this by good works or by being good enough. No one is good enough. You get this by believing in Him and accepting the gift of grace. You become redeemed by His payment on the cross.

So the first step for establishing a God-based vision for your life is to acknowledge that you believe in Jesus. Then reach out to Him in prayer and ask Him to help you know Him more. It doesn't have to be a special prayer, just a reaching out from your heart to His. If you haven't reached out to God this way before, now is a good time to pause and do that.

Put your prayer in your own words. Ask Him to come into your life. Accept that He died for your sins and your separation from God. Express that you don't want to be separated and that you want His help. Ask for His grace and peace and accept it.

He loves you. He longs to know you and wants you to know Him.

> *Call to me and I will answer you and tell you great and unsearchable things you do not know.*
> *Jeremiah 33:3*

As your relationship with God grows through your day-to-day study of the Scriptures and prayer, you will capture the vision of what He has planned for your life. He knew you before you were in your mother's womb. He has dreams for your life, too. As you learn your identity in Christ and who God says you are, your vision for life expands and gets bigger.

Thank you for coming on this journey with us. We are excited to walk it out with you as you seek God for His vision for your life.

— *Wendy and Yvonne*

Notes for Bible Study Leaders

This study (completed at the suggested pace) takes 4 weeks to complete, spending about ½ hour a day for 5 days a week. You'll need a total of 5 weekly meetings, including the first meeting where you will explain how the study works and discuss the Introduction.

As a leader, you should choose a day and time that the group will come together to meet each week. The participants will be responsible for going through the 5 days of study each week on their own.

You can do this study as a in-person group study, or it can be done as an online study. Some choose to meet through an online webinar forum from their homes. Contact us through our contact page at HolyScents.org if you need guidance with this format. While leading the study, we recommend that you do the following to help your study flow well.

1. Choose a date to start the study. Give yourself several weeks so that you can order the books and the oils in time. Announce that you are doing the study. Give everyone the link to order the study online at (GrowingHealthyHomes.com or HolyScents.org), or you can collect the money from everyone and order all the copies yourself. Give a date that everyone needs to order by so that they have their books in time. Please order a copy for each participant.

2. Get your oils ordered in time to receive them before the first day of your study. You may choose to have people order their oils individually, or you may place one order for all of them and possibly save on shipping.

3. On the first meeting day, we suggest a prayer to open the meeting. Then give an overview of the study and walk everyone through the Introduction of this book.

Take some time to teach about the particular oil you will be using in this study. Look up the qualities of Envision™ (or Frankincense), and make sure everyone knows multiple uses for the oil and how it may benefit them in other areas of their lives. Use this meeting to teach the basics of essential oil usage, and if time allows, expand on the importance of purity. Instruct them on what to do if they get oil in an eye or other sensitive area. All of this is covered in the Introduction, so just use the Introduction as your notes for leading the first class. Explain that participants will have homework five days a week. Explain that they will be making a vision board, and encourage them to decide what kind of board they want (cork board, poster board, or even simply a piece of paper). Encourage them to gather the materials for their vision board ahead of time. Express care and concern for your study members. Take prayer requests, and end in prayer.

4. After the first meeting, faithfully meet the same time/ day each week with your study members for 4 more weeks and review the material that was studied each week. Pray to open your meeting. Read parts of the study out loud (what stuck out to you?) and ask people to share what they learned. Did the Holy Spirit reveal anything? Did anyone sense God was speaking to them? How so? What really spoke to them? What does smelling the oil do to them emotionally? How does it affect them? Do they like the smell? Do they feel calmer when breathing it? Do they feel closer to God? What is one goal that they wrote down and would they be willing to share about it? Have people share about things they learned about themselves and what nuggets they mined out of their hearts each week. At the end of the study, remind participants to complete their vision boards and bring them to share at the final meeting.

5. On the final week, ask participants to share something they learned about themselves during this study. How has this process helped them to narrow down the vision for their lives? Did they learn anything? After your discussions, ask people to show their vision boards and to pick a few things from it that they are willing to share. Thank them for being a participant, answer any questions, and remind them to visit us at HolyScents.org and click on the "feedback" tab so that they can leave us feedback on the study. End in prayer and congratulate everyone for completing the study and creating their board.

For more leader tips, tools and other topical Bible studies, visit us online at:

HolyScents.org
or
https://www.facebook.com/HolyScents/

The Study

24

To Perish or Succeed

WEEK 1
DAY 1

Proverbs 29:18 (KJV)
"Where there is no vision the people perish."

STEP 1: Meditating on God's Word
With Aromatherapy

If you have a diffuser, get it out and add your Envision™ or Frankincense oil to it. According to the directions that came with your diffuser, run it close to yourself the whole time you are doing this study so that you can smell the aroma of the oil. Diffusers are designed to get the oil molecules into the air where you can breathe them in easily. If you don't have a diffuser, you can become a human diffuser! Put several drops of oil into your hands, rub your hands together and cup them over your nose. Take a few minutes and get still. Breathe the scent in deeply. When you are calm and relaxed, move your attention to the scripture for this week, Proverbs 29:18.

Continue to breathe in the aroma while meditating on the above scripture for about 5 minutes. Take your time. Relax. Let the scented molecules travel up the olfactory nerve in your nose and cross your blood/brain barrier. Deep breathing gets the oil into your bloodstream where you want it. The oil molecules affect and stimulate the limbic center of your brain where your emotions are processed. As this area is stimulated each day during this study, your brain will begin to associate this smell with the topic of

How do you meditate on the scripture? To do it effectively you need to be hungry for God and expect to hear from the Holy Spirit! Ask the Holy Spirit to help you search out God's revelation to you of the scripture you are studying. He is faithful to do it.

Vision and the scriptures you are meditating on!

Repeat the scripture *out loud* slowly, continually breathing in the aroma. Ask yourself what this scripture means. Contemplate what it might mean for you. Imagine yourself with clear direction and understanding of the direction you should walk in life for the next 5 to 10 years. Then compare that vision with an image of yourself with no vision at all, wandering aimlessly through life from situation to situation. Which image gives life to you? Which one gives hope and a future? Which would you rather have? Clear direction is always the best! Knowing which way to walk for the next 5-10 years is powerful. Can you even imagine if you had vision for the next 20 years of your life? It is possible. Through this study, we will help you develop that vision!

STEP 2: Read and Respond

Continue to diffuse your oil; or put a few fresh drops on your hands, rub together and cup over your nose to inhale the scent while you read the devotional below.

To Perish or Succeed?

BY WENDY SELVIG

Statistics show that most people don't make long-term plans and goals. It's said that about 80 percent of people never set goals for themselves. Brian Tracy, a popular business speaker and motivator, says that people generally don't know how to set goals. He says that goals need to be clear, written, specific and measurable.

Some people set short-term goals like finishing college or losing weight. But to look into the future and set firm life goals for more than a few years down the road is almost unheard of. Scripture tells us that, "Without a vision the people perish," (Proverbs 29:18). So how many people are on that road of perishing? How many never know their true calling, purpose and identity? I'll tell you. Those who do not realize God's vision for their lives and who do not have written goals and steps about how to achieve that vision.

Did you know that God knew you before you were in your mother's womb (Jeremiah 1:5)? He thought of you and planned how you would fit into the picture of humanity. Did you know that God created you with a purpose in mind? I believe it with all of my heart. You may not think that highly of yourself, but God does. His ways are higher than our ways; His thoughts higher than our thoughts (Isaiah 55:9).

Psalm 139:16 says, "Your eyes have seen my unformed substance; And in Your book were all written the days that were ordained for me, When as yet there was not one of them." This scripture tells us that God has ordained days for us. He has a vision for our lives. Wouldn't it be awesome to find out to what purposes you are called?

Wouldn't it be great to find out what He was thinking when He made you?

Proverbs 25:2 says that, "It is the glory of God to conceal a matter, but the glory of kings is to search out a matter." 1 Peter 2:9 and Revelation 1:6 call us kings and priests of God's Kingdom. Hello king! Your job is to rule, reign and to search out His purpose and plan for your life. He has hidden treasure and jewels within you that reveal His purposes. You have to mine them and search them out of your heart to find them.

The funny thing about God... He doesn't always reveal His purpose and plans easily. Have you noticed? I think He likes for us to seek Him. In fact, I know He does. He wants you to search Him out! As you search, you are seeking, asking and trusting Him. You are growing in your relationship with Him, and that is precisely what He wants. The process of finding your purpose involves finding Him. He wants to be found. He wants to be included in the revealing of your purpose. He loves you so much. Here are a few more scriptures to support these thoughts.

"Ask and it will be given to you; seek and you will find; knock and the door will be opened to you."
Matthew 7:7

"For I know the plans I have for you," declares the Lord, "plans to prosper you and not to harm you, plans to give you hope and a future. Then you will call upon me and come and pray to me, and I will listen to you. You will seek me and find me when you seek me with all your heart."
Jeremiah 29:11-13

"Trust in the Lord and do good; dwell in the land and enjoy safe pasture. Delight yourself in the Lord and he will give you the desires of your heart. Commit your way to the Lord; trust in

him and he will do this: He will make your righteousness shine like the dawn, the justice of your cause like the noonday sun."
Psalms 37:3-6

God has definite plans for your life, but it's your job to search them out. We are going to take the next few weeks to help you in that search. We are going to ask questions and stir up your thinking to help you to draw a picture that will show the plans and purposes He has for you. You will likely find some general directions on some topics and specific directions in others. It is a process, and you have to mine these jewels out of your heart like a miner digs jewels out of the earth. We are excited to help you do a little digging. Whatever you find will help define your purpose more and determine a future you can pursue with confidence.

Is there a specific area in your life that you would like to find God's purpose for during this study? We will cover many areas, but maybe one in particular is standing out to you: vocation, serving, family, finances, relationships, etc. Identify one area in which you are seeking God for direction above all others and write it in the space below:

If you need help writing a prayer, first address the Heavenly Father (Dear Father). Then thank Him for something in your life. Next, ask Him to reveal His plans and purposes for your life as you search these things out. Ask Him for the grace to understand and to hear His voice and direction for the specific area in which you are seeking direction. Then as John 14:13-14 suggests, end the prayer "in Jesus' name". Praying in Jesus' name means praying with His authority and asking God the Father to act upon our prayers because we come in the name of His Son, Jesus.

Step 3: Journal and Pray

Continue to diffuse or inhale your oil as you write down your thoughts about the scriptures we have studied today. If you are smelling your oil from your hands, put a dab of fresh oil right under your nose so that you can breathe the scent while you use your hands for writing. Write down a prayer asking for help and revelation for the specific area you wrote down before.

_____

_____

_____

_____

_____

_____

_____

_____

_____

_____

_____

_____

_____

_____

Writing Down the Vision

WEEK 1
DAY 2

Proverbs 29:18 (KJV)
"Where there is no vision the people perish."

STEP 1: Meditating on God's Word With Aromatherapy

Every day of this study, we will begin by getting the essential oils into our body. You may choose to diffuse or breathe in your oil. We will also introduce other ways to use your oil, but diffusing is always a good option. Today, in addition to diffusing, let's add a topical application. Get your diffuser running with your oil, as you did yesterday. Then apply 1 drop of oil on the inside of each wrist. The oil will enter your blood stream through your veins as well as through your nose as you inhale it. Close your eyes and repeat the scripture slowly and out loud, continually breathing in the aroma.

Let's meditate on the meaning of the word "vision" today. The word vision in the Amplified Bible is translated as "divine guidance, revelation of God and His Word." And the word "perish" is translated as "the people are unrestrained". Another translation says that to perish is "to be made naked". To be made naked is to remove the clothing, or the protection, on your body. Could having a vision for the future protect your life, as clothing protects a body?

3 1

Slow your thoughts and think about how these words apply to your life, allowing the Holy Spirit to speak to you and guide your thoughts as you continue to breathe in your oil. Meditating on the Word of God is powerful, for the words are living and active and full of power. They are sharper than a two-edged sword and divide between the soul and spirit, joints and marrow. The Word exposes our innermost thoughts and desires! (Hebrews 4:12) Meditate on this week's scripture, allowing it to expose any fears or doubts you have about this topic of vision or about your life.

STEP 2: Read and Respond

Continue to breathe in your oil while you read below. Diffuse or put a drop under your nose so that you smell it.

Writing Down the Vision

BY YVONNE PACE & WENDY SELVIG

Let's look at Habakkuk 2:2: "Then the Lord said to me, "Write the vision down on tablets that a herald may run with it."" In this scripture, God told the prophet Habakkuk to write down the vision that He had for the people of Israel. God wanted it written down so that others could see it.

Do you know what is really neat about Habakkuk writing down his vision? It brought God's will from heaven to the earth. The physical act of writing it down actually brought it from the realm of heaven to the earth! Writing it down made it clear for those on earth to see it and know what it was. This act made it possible for someone to run with it and make it happen. Could this principle be the same today for the vision of your life? Could writing down our goals and dreams bring heaven's possibilities into the earthly realm?

If you write down the vision, not only will you see it but others will see it as well. You will have searched God, found what you believe His will for your life is, and materialized it onto paper on the earth. This is bringing the vision from heaven's realm to the earth. *This will give you a starting place for making the vision come to pass in your life. And maybe even heralds will run to help bring it to pass!*

While smelling your chosen essential oil, ask yourself the following questions. (Record your responses in the spaces below the questions):

1. How do the scriptures we have discussed thus far make you feel about your present life situation?

_____

_____

_____

_____

2. Do you have a vision for your future?

_____

_____

_____

_____

3. Do you believe God is powerful enough and detailed enough to have plans for your life? Are you ready to find out what they are?

4. What might you learn from what Solomon says about not having a vision (Proverbs 29:18)? What might come of your future if you do not have one?

5. What might you learn from what God instructed Habakkuk to do in writing down the vision that God gave him to share with the people of Israel?

6. How might your future benefit from having a written vision?

Application

We want to introduce you to the idea of making a vision board. This will be a board that you hang in your office, your bedroom or any wall of your choice. It is a place to put things you want to accomplish or problems you would like to solve. You may include ideas that you come up with during this study. The weekly reviews will provide you with material to add to your board. When you finish your vision board, you'll have a more complete picture of God's vision for your life. We hope to help draw out these things from your heart and help you see what God has planted within you.

Gathering Materials

First of all, decide what you want your vision board to be made out of. You can get a corkboard at any hobby store. You could use a white board or even an inexpensive poster board or a white piece of paper. Once you have decided what you are going to use, go purchase or gather your supplies. If you use a piece of paper, you can tack it to a hanging corkboard later if desired.

At the end of each week, we will be writing out vision statements for each area of life we have studied. Then, in the final days of the study, we will cut them out (or make photocopies and cut them out) and paste or tack them to your vision board. You can get creative and cut words out of magazines. Consider different fonts, colors and textures from your computer to make it interesting. Be as creative (or not) as you choose! We have more ideas in the final study day of this book for making your board attractive. Do you have some basic ideas of what might be a part of your vision? Don't worry if you don't yet.

While you are diffusing your essential oil, prepare your heart for the journey that is coming over the next few weeks and thank the Lord that He will help you. We will start gathering firm ideas tomorrow. Today is a day of thankfulness and gratitude for this journey. Thank Him that He will be faithful to speak and show you His vision for your life over the next few weeks. Have faith that He has a vision for your life and that you are about to find out what it looks like.

STEP 3: Journal and Pray

If you have received any ideas today about the vision for your life, begin to brainstorm about them. They might be single words or phrases. Don't feel pressured to come up with something really solid. Continue to breathe in your oil blend and write any ideas that may have come to mind today. Tomorrow we will dig in and get more specific about your vision.

_____

_____

_____

_____

_____

_____

_____

End with Prayer: "Lord, I am excited and expectant of the plans that you will be revealing to me over the next few days and weeks. I understand that your Word is powerful and active in me now and in the days to come so that I can discover all that You want to share with me. I give you praise and thanks, In Jesus' name, amen."

When God Takes Up Your Cause

WEEK 1
DAY 3

Proverbs 29:18 (KJV)
"Where there is no vision the people perish."
(Latin Vulgate)

STEP 1: Meditating on God's Word With Aromatherapy

Diffuse your oil in a diffuser or put it in your hands and cup them over your mouth and nose, breathing in the scent for at least 3-5 minutes. We are on day three of this study, and we are meditating on the same scripture for the first 5 days. While it may seem repetitious, today take note of where you find this scripture in the Bible. See if you can memorize Proverbs 29:18 so that you will remember where to find it later. Recall all of the things that you have thought about so far while meditating on this verse. Relax. Be calm. Breathe in the scent, and meditate on the scripture above.

The Vulgate Latin version of this scripture interprets the words "no vision" as "no prophecy." According to the Cambridge Bible for Schools and Colleges commentaries, prophecy is the contact between God and the human spirit, where God communicates with us. So, for practical understanding, you could say, "without God's communication with us, we perish."

As you complete this study, seek God for wisdom and insight about your future. You want to hear from Him and nobody else. It's *His* insight and *His* direction that will give you hope and a future. It's *His* communication that will keep you from perishing.

STEP 2: Read and Respond

Continue to diffuse and breathe your oil as you read this next section.

When God Takes Up Your Cause

BY WENDY SELVIG

God has given us some keys to finding the vision and plan He has for us. One of them is found in Psalm 37:4-6:

Delight yourself in the Lord and he will give you the desires of your heart. Commit your way to the Lord; trust in him and he will do this: He will make your righteousness shine like the dawn, the justice of your cause like the noonday sun.

What are the desires of your heart? Do you even know what they are? Some of us haven't thought about our desires for a long time. Many people's desires lay undeveloped and hidden. Many people never see the desires of their hearts fulfilled. I believe that is a tragedy. Romans 11:29 says, "For God's gifts and his call are irrevocable." That means that whether or not you believe or trust in Him, the gifts He put in you are real and are yours. They are not given to you based on whether you have relationship with Him or not. Your gifts are from God to help you in your life. Your gifts and your desires are often from the same cloth; they are intertwined.

The Bible declares that God wants to give you the desires of your heart. God built our desires into us, and they make us unique. They lead us toward the purpose He has for us, whether they are secular or spiritual. For example, perhaps you are a gifted businessperson. God has gifted you and put desires for business within you because those gifts have to do with the callings and purposes *He* has planned for you.

Some people think that only full-time ministers are working for God. Friend, life is ministry. You don't need a title. Don't discount your gifts and desires because they serve you outside of the title of "ministry." Most CEO's could be an apostle in the church environment. They are the vision people, the big-picture people. They are starters with desires to start either businesses or churches. The gifting is the same. Most human resource directors could also be pastors. Their gift directs them to shepherding people, within the church or outside it. Evangelists are great salespersons. Don't discount the field you are in if it is not in a "ministry". Your field of choice; the one you love to be in, the one you are good at, has to do with the purpose God is calling you to and the gifts He has put inside of you. You can use your gifts to honor God inside or outside the church.

God wants you to have your desires, but according to Psalms 37 you have to do two things. *You have to delight yourself in the Lord, and commit your way to Him.* What does that say to me? It suggests that I have to be in relationship with Him (and love Him) and make a commitment to make my plans honor Him, no matter what. And you know what? He gets behind plans like that! He will help me succeed.

He is a King and He rules over the Kingdom of God that is more real than the earth plane we currently live in. He is not a president; He is a King. And He wants to have deep relationship with you. He wants you to TRUST Him and commit your ways (your vision and dream) to Him.

Proverbs 16:9 says, "In their hearts humans plan their course, but the LORD establishes their steps." We plan our course, often in line with the desires of our hearts. We have some say in the path we choose. But God establishes our steps as we walk them out in faith. When He is our partner, He shows us how to walk and how to bring those dreams to light. He illuminates the path and makes success possible!

Commit your way to the LORD; trust in him and he will do this: He will make your righteous reward shine like the dawn, your vindication like the noonday sun.
Psalm 37:5-7

Notice He doesn't say, "Commit the Lord's way to Him..." It says, "Commit your way" to the Lord. Your way. Your. Way. Commit *your way* to Him and trust in Him. Notice he also doesn't say, "the justice of His cause..." He says, "the justice of your cause." Your vision. Your dream. Your cause.

What you are fighting for? When you love Him and trust Him with your cause, He will make your cause shine like the noonday sun. That is how you accomplish a vision... through relationship with the Lord and trusting Him to be involved. You commit your way to Him and let Him make the justice of your cause to shine like the noonday sun! Do you have a clear vision for your life? Do you know what God's plan and purposes for you are? Would you like to know? We're going to begin digging for some of the jewels that are hidden within your heart today, in order to start shaping your vision.

Application

If you could solve any world problem, what would it be? Think big right now, bigger than your personal life. What world issue bugs you the most? Here are a few examples: Aids/HIV, sex trafficking, world hunger, terrorism, pure drinking water for all, refugees, unemployment, obesity, etc....

If you have never thought about these problems as something that is seriously an issue for you, start considering them now. What bothers you the most? Read through the issues listed and choose the one that pops off the page the most for you. For today, expand your focus to that world problem. You don't have to come up with a solution, just identify the issue that bothers you the most. Write the issue in the space below:

_____

_____

_____

_____

_____

_____

_____

_____

_____

_____

_____

_____

STEP 3: Journal and Pray

As you continue to diffuse and smell your essential oil, reflect on the issue you have written above. If God wanted to use you to help end or solve this problem, would you be willing to follow His calling? Write a prayer below and include some or all of the following ideas:

• Express your desire to know Him more and to love Him.

• Commit your way to Him so that He is in control.

• Express your desire to trust Him.

• Thank Him for highlighting an issue in this world that you are willing to be a part of if He leads you that way.

• Commit to make a difference where you can.

Use the lines below to write your prayer down. Make a record of it. Today is a big day in your journey. It is the day you engaged the Father and committed your way and plan to Him, that it might succeed.

TODAY'S DATE: _____

_____

_____

_____

_____

_____

_____

_____

_____

_____

Making A Local Impact

WEEK 1
DAY 4

Proverbs 29:18 (KJV)
"Where there is no vision the people perish."

STEP 1: Meditating on God's Word
With Aromatherapy

Diffuse your oil or rub a drop under each nostril of your nose. If your skin is sensitive, remember to add a little carrier oil (Young Living's V-6™ blend is best, but coconut or olive oil will do in a pinch). Make sure you meditate while breathing the scent for at least 3-5 minutes.

Can you close your eyes and recall where this scripture is found? Try doing that and see if you can remember the scripture reference. You don't have to memorize it, but lets try. Here's a little trick: Do you know anyone who is 29 years old? Where did you live and what were you doing when you were 29? How about when you were 18? Think about that now and repeat the scripture reference and the scripture.

Reflect again on the idea of perishing versus walking forward with vision for your life. What does it look like to perish? Could it be just floating from circumstance to circumstance, wherever life may take you?

Life is busy and all consuming at times. It's hard to know when to say yes and when to say no. When you know

4 3

who you are and what your vision and purpose is, you can confidently say no to the things that don't line up with this plan. When things come into your life that do line up with your vision, you can say yes to them. Understanding yourself and your vision will help you to be laser-focused in regard to responding to life's situations and opportunities.

STEP 2: Read and Respond

What is Your VISION For Your Local Town or Community?

BY YVONNE PACE

Do you have a passion about any issue that impacts your community? Are you ready to take action to make your town or city a better place? Civic engagement is something we all should consider. Working in a soup kitchen, serving on a neighborhood association, writing letters to elected officials, fund-raising for charity, running for political office, voting, persuading others to vote, protesting a worthy cause, picking up trash along a highway, etc.: these are all examples of civic engagement.

Start thinking about how you could make a difference in your local community. When you make a significant impact your community, you are doing your part to make the world a better place for everyone. What part of the community would you like to see made better? Think about the local civic needs. Is there any area that sticks out to you that needs improvement?

Consider your natural abilities and talents and how you could use them to assist your community. What skills do you already have (or what skills could you attain fairly easily) to help out somewhere? Who is on your heart the most? How can you make a difference for that group of people? For example, do you have a heart to work with the elderly? Maybe you could get your CDL license so that you could drive a senior citizen's van on the weekends. Taking people who are no longer able to drive to the grocery store is a community need and ministry. Prayerfully research the local civic needs in your community as a starting point to inspire your heart!

It's easy to accept the idea that one person can't make a very big difference, but this isn't true. Let me tell you a popular story. There once was a boy standing on a beach where thousands of starfish had washed up onto the shore. The little boy was throwing the starfish back into the water to try to save them. It was obvious he couldn't save them all, so a man walking along the beach approached him and said, "Why throw them back? You can't possibly make a difference!" The little boy looked up, picked up a starfish and threw it into the water and said, "Made a difference for that one!" Every life we touch, and every place we get involved makes a difference and makes the world better. Even more, when we follow the Holy Spirit's prompting to get involved, we walk in the love of Christ to reach those who need ministry today.

Application
Who in your community does your heart lean towards helping? Write your answer in the space below.

_____

_____

_____

What natural abilities/certifications do you have that you could put to use in your community? Take a few minutes to write your thoughts into a list:

1. _____

2. _____

3. _____

4. _____

5. _____

Take your time. Come back to this list later in the day or tomorrow and re-read what you have written, allowing the Holy Spirit to bring things to your remembrance. Another tool you can use to recognize your abilities is personality testing. You can take a personality test online or go to your local library and find the DiSC (Dominance, Influence, Steadiness, and Conscientiousness) or Jung test to increase your awareness to your own personality as it is defined in psychology. You can take a spiritual gift test as well; many are available on the Internet. It is recommended that you take these types of tests periodically to see how your gifts develop over time. Consider your personality and gift set and think about how you might serve an area of your community.

Are there one or two local/city/state issues that you would get involved with if you had the resources and time? If so, write the names of the issue/s in the space below:

_____

_____

_____

_____

Step 3: Journal and Pray

It's time to gather your thoughts and make decisions about how you might help your community. Even if you don't have the time to do it right now, imagine you had extra hours in your week. How would you get involved? What area gets you excited to help?

Take a few minutes and find the words or phrases that describe your thoughts about your community. Write your thoughts in the space below:

_____

_____

_____

End with a prayer. You can follow the sample here or come up your own. *"My Lord Jesus, I ask You to bring to my remembrance the gifts You have given me over my life. As I meditate on Your Word, thank You for showing me the gifts that You want me to develop as I delight myself in You today. Let me see the experiences that I have had, even before I knew You as my Savior and up to the present day, both positive and negative; and may these experiences become clear to me now and in the days going forward. I know all these gifts and experiences can be used for Your glory. I love You Lord, and I pray this in Jesus' name, amen (so be it)!"*

Write your own prayer here:

_____

_____

_____

_____

_____

Week 1 Review & Meditation

WEEK 1

DAY 5

STEP 1: Meditating on God's Word With Aromatherapy

Today is a day for reinforcing all that you've learned this week. Diffuse your oil blend or put a few drops under your nose and breathe the scent while you complete today's lesson.

Take time to flip through the past few days of your journal and note taking and review your thoughts and prayers. Take 3-5 minutes to reflect on the weekly scripture. How does this scripture apply to your life? Were you able to memorize it? Write it out here:

_____

_____

_____

_____

STEP 2: Writing Down Your Vision

On the next page you will see some boxes. You will complete these in each weekly review, and at the end of this study you will use the answers you have written in the boxes to complete your vision board.

Write your answers in the boxes provided:

1. What cause or world problem bothers you the most? What issue would you like to help solve? Write your answer in the box below. You can write simple words like, "World Hunger," or you can write out a complete sentence such as, "I want to help end world hunger."

My Vision For My Community:

2. Is there a local issue in your city or state that you would like to see resolved? Write the issue in the box below.

My Vision For The World:

3. While still diffusing and breathing in your oil, write out a prayer that engages the Father about these issues. Tell Him if you'd like to be a part of the solution. Commit your ways in these areas to Him.

Vision For Your Family

WEEK 2
DAY 1

Psalm 37:4-5 (NKJV)
"Delight yourself also in the Lord, And He shall give you the desires of your heart. Commit your way to the Lord, Trust also in Him, And He shall bring it to pass."

STEP 1: Meditating on God's Word With Aromatherapy

This is the first day of week two, and we are meditating on a new scripture this week. Diffuse your oil or rub it under your nose. Make sure you are breathing the scent while meditating on Psalm 37:4-5. Close your eyes. Slow your breathing. Take deep breaths of the wonderful aroma.

Today while you are thinking about this scripture, think about the loved ones in your life and how this scripture may apply to them. If you develop a plan and vision for your life for the next five years, how will it improve their lives? What if you had some plans in place for the next 10-15 years?! How would that affect everyone?

A good person leaves an inheritance for their children's children, but a sinner's wealth is stored up for the righteous.
Proverbs 13:22

When we live without a plan and we have no vision, it is hard to leave anything for anyone. Whether it is a financial, spiritual, emotional, or physical inheritance, we have

5 1

to plan to make that happen. While you are meditating on this word, ask the Lord to give you ideas about how you might leave an inheritance for your children and grandchildren. An inheritance may be financial, but it may also be spiritual or emotional. Ask Him to show you the potential for you to impact your future generations for the better.

STEP 2: Read and Respond

Continue to diffuse your oil or put a few fresh drops on your hands, rubbing them together and cupping over your nose to inhale the scent while you read below.

What Is Your Vision for Your Family?

BY YVONNE PACE & WENDY SELVIG

What does the word "family" mean to you? Some people are born into big families with lots of activity; others are born as only children into quiet, and possibly more structured environments. Some are adopted; some are estranged. Some families are strong and supportive; others are broken and hurting. The one thing we all have in common is that we cannot choose the family into which we were born.

Your family has it's own unique challenges. There may be hurts, unmet expectations and wounds associated with your family. On the other hand, you may have wonderful memories and a good foundation associated with your family. Whatever your individual circumstance, the family you grew up in molded and shaped how you see life. If you come from a family that is broken and you have incurred wounds, you may need to receive healing for those wounds so that you can move forward in a healthy way with your current or future family. Sometimes we need a little more physical action on our part to bring healing for family relationships. If this means seeking out a licensed counselor, do it. If it means drawing boundary lines with unhealthy individuals, do it. If it means forgiving and moving forward, do it.

The good news is that Jesus has provided healing for us in all things! (2 Corinthians 1:20) That healing includes the healing of relationships as we diligently seek Him. Consider spending time in prayer so the Lord can speak to you about how to begin the healing process for relationships in your family. Make sure to write down any thoughts you have while praying. He speaks to us in our thoughts, and sometimes we think they are our own, when really it is the Lord who is guiding us.

Mark 11:25 instructs that when you pray, you should first forgive anyone you are holding a grudge against so that your Father in Heaven will forgive your sins as well. Forgiveness is something we should all practice as we work with our family members.

It can also help to find a prayer partner to agree in prayer for your family too. Matthew 18:19-20 says that where two agree in prayer our Father in heaven will be in their midst. Find someone who is willing to pray for your family with you because two are stronger than one. Also remember that Romans 8:34 promises us that Jesus is at the right hand of the Father interceding for us! Jesus is our main prayer partner! Finding another to pray with us is powerful, but including Jesus makes *three* who are praying and agreeing together! That is powerful prayer from which you should expect to see answers!

Another part of our family life is the people *we choose* to bring into our family. Sometimes we choose other adults to look to as fathers or mothers (when needed). We choose intimate friendships. We choose spouses. We choose whether or not to have children. Some choose animals to be part of their family. All of these loved ones are our choice, our family...and we are responsible to love and look after them. As these people have been grafted into the vine of our lives, how can we plan so that they flourish and grow because of us? How can we ensure a more stable future for them because of us?

Think about the people in your life that you consider family. What can you do to better their lives for the next 5 years? What would you like to see accomplished for them in the next 10 to 15 years? What about 40 to 50 years from now? Can you comprehend that far into the future? In the next section, journal the answers to these questions and consider how having a vision for your family may impact their future. May the Lord give you inspiration as you discover the vision He has for you and your family!

Application

Answer the following questions for each person in your family whom you want to impact.

1. Is this family member spiritually healthy? Does he or she have a relationship with Jesus? Is there anything you can plan to do for him/her over the coming years that might make a difference in his/her spiritual future? (Consider speaking scriptures over this person's life and praying for him/her as a start.)

_____

_____

2. Is this family member financially stable? Will he or she be financially stable in 5-10 years on his/her current path? Is there anything you could do to help

this person financially? (You might consider starting a savings account or buying something for him/her that will retain its value.)

_____

_____

3. Is this family member a child or a youth? If so, what can you teach him or her about money? What can you teach him or her about God?

_____

_____

4. Whether or not you have financial stability and/or freedom, your loved ones need to see and experience love and joy. What can you plan to do to help members of your family to experience love and joy from you?

_____

_____

5. Do you have a way of providing an inheritance for your children? Did you know that a Young Living business can provide a source of income that you can build slowly and is will-able to your children? You can find out more from your Bible Study leader or at HolyScents.org. (You can also find the income disclosure statement from Young Living there.)

As you continue to think about vision for your family, pause and commit your vision to the Lord with a prayer to bring His plan into focus.

"Heavenly Father, thank You for my family. Help me to capture Your vision for my future and my family. Help me to see them 10 years from now, 20 years from now, and even 50 years from now. How can I help and bless them? How can I work towards leaving a legacy for my children and their children? Help me to see what You have planned for my family. In Jesus' name, amen."

Now, review the answers you gave to the previous questions. What action steps stand out that you can do for your family in the next few years? Write a summary of the action steps you plan to take below *(This will also be what you write in the "Vision for Family" box for this week's review.)*:

_____

_____

_____

_____

_____

STEP 3: Journal and Pray

Journal about your family. Write about what it currently looks like and what you wish it to be. Commit your family to the Lord and ask Him to intervene in your loved ones' lives. Ask Him to help you provide help spiritually and financially, that you may leave an inheritance for them.

_____

_____

_____

_____

_____

Vision for Your Vocation

WEEK 2
DAY 2

Psalm 37:4-5 (NKJV)
"Delight yourself also in the Lord, And He shall give
you the desires of your heart. Commit your way to the
Lord, Trust also in Him, And He shall bring it to pass."

STEP 1: Meditating on God's Word
With Aromatherapy

Diffuse your essential oil or put a dab under both nostrils, breathing it in.

Spend 3-5 minutes breathing this aroma and thinking about the scripture. Get still, and think about what each word means and how it applies to you.

You are teaching your brain to associate scriptures about vision with the scent of your oil. In the future when you are praying for vision, get out your oil and smell it while you ask God for help. The blend will help your brain recall scriptures you have hidden in your heart, as your brain will have made associations with the topic through your study and meditation.

STEP 2: Read and Respond

Continue to diffuse or inhale the scent as you read this next section.

Your Gift Makes The Way

BY WENDY SELVIG

What is your dream vocation? Many would say that a dream job is one you love so much that you'd do it for free. That kind of job satisfaction can only be found when you are using your natural gifts and talents: the things that God put in you to help you on your path of life. Gifts come easily and are enjoyable; that's how you know they're gifts.

If you aren't currently in a dream job, don't despair. Even if you aren't passionate about your job, if it supplies stable income for your family, don't feel like you have to quit to chase your dream. You can still live your dream by developing your gifts and talents outside of your occupation.

Ask the Lord to show you how you can serve Him with your gifts in other ways. When you serve in your gifted area, you develop your gift. Over time, a developed gift becomes valuable and makes a way for you (Proverbs 18:16)! Focus on developing your gift to a master level and it will open doors! If you develop your gift now, it may become your dream job later!

One of my gifts is artistic creativity. I can express that in multiple ways. I grew up taking photos and expressing myself through photography for fun. It was a hobby that I loved so much. As my friends started getting married, they often hired me to photograph their weddings for an income. They were aware of my gift and wanted my services because my gift had already gone before me. They had seen my photography and liked what they saw.

Maybe you could start a side business with your gift someday. Are you a great organizer? Develop that gift.

Help friends organize their garages and closets for free. Offer to serve your church by organizing anything that needs it. Work towards getting a reputation for doing it well. At some point, you will have history and a track record that will make a way for you to use your gifting as a side business. Your business could take off and one day replace your current job! Become a master at your gift so that it makes a way for you.

Do you love natural health? Do you love essential oils? You could hold essential oils classes and Bible studies like this one, helping people to find natural health solutions while creating a steady stream of extra income for your family. I used Young Living essential oils for 3 years before ever considering it as a business. My passion for natural health and the results I saw from people using the oils naturally pulled me into a business, and I started to receive paychecks for pursuing my passion. Now I've replaced the income I was making at my regular job with my Young Living income. My developed passion and gift made a way. (An income disclosure statement is available online at HolyScents.org under "For Leaders.")

So I want to ask you a question: Do you know what your gifts are? Rest assured that God has given you at least one (or two or three or more)! Separate your thoughts from your vocation right now and just think about your gifts and passions. What are you good at? It might be cooking. It might be understanding nutrition. It might be gardening. It might be cleaning, or it might be listening well to others. Maybe you are good at organizing. Maybe you're a good mother or father or spouse. Maybe your gift is praying. Maybe it is starting businesses. What are you good at?

Take a few minutes and list at least 5 things you believe you are gifted at or passionate about. What do you enjoy doing?

1. _____

2. _____

3. _____

4. _____

5. _____

Now, choose one of the items from your list and write three things you can begin to do to develop that gift:

1. _____

2. _____

3. _____

Now write one or two places you can volunteer or give your time that would give you experience developing your gift. If your gift is something like a musical talent, it requires practice. Write one or two things you can do to get that practice. Make it an action step.

1. _____

2. _____

When you are skilled in an area, your gifting makes room for you. If you are good and get better and better, you will eventually become an expert, and people will want your advice. They will want to see how you do it. There will be room for ministry and for blessing people. You will bring your gift to the world as a contribution to mankind.

If you don't develop your gifts, you'll never know what God really has for you.

The thief cometh not, but for to steal, and to kill,
and to destroy: I am come that they might have life,
and that they might have it more abundantly."
John 10:10

He has a wonderful life for you. He comes to give you life, and give it more abundantly. Your life will be abundant when you are walking in the gifts He has put inside of you. So take time to find and develop your gifts.

STEP 3: Journal and Pray

As you continue to diffuse and smell your essential oil, reflect on the gifts God has given you. Take time today to thank Him for the gifts He has given you. Make a plan for how you will develop these gifts. Journal your prayer below:

_____

_____

_____

_____

_____

_____

_____

_____

_____

_____

62

Vision for Your Spiritual Life

WEEK 2
DAY 3

Psalm 37:4-5 (NKJV)
"Delight yourself also in the Lord, And He shall give
you the desires of your heart. Commit your way to the
Lord, Trust also in Him, And He shall bring it to pass."

STEP 1: Meditating on God's Word With Aromatherapy

Diffuse your essential oil or put it in your hands and cup over your mouth and nose, breathing it in. Spend 3-5 minutes breathing this scent and thinking about the scripture above. Get still, and think about what each word means and how it applies to you. Allow yourself to slow down. Get quiet. Take a few deep breaths. Meditation requires purposefully getting yourself to a restful state.

STEP 2: Read and Respond

Make sure your diffuser is still running and you are breathing in your essential oil while reading the following devotional. If you don't have a diffuser, you may put a few drops of oil under each nostril.

Going Deeper With God
(A life that leaks God's power and presence)

A TESTIMONY BY WENDY SELVIG

*"For the eyes of the LORD move to and fro
throughout the earth that He may strongly support
those whose heart is completely His"
2 Chronicles 16:9a (NASB)*

I love the Lord with all my heart. My faith in His promises and love is strong. I have seen Him interact in my world in response to my faith, and it has confirmed His existence, His goodness, and His love in my life. I wasn't born with this strong of faith; it grew over the course of many years of searching and honestly looking for Him. But as I've searched, He has supported and answered me. I'm certain He will answer you too. He loves to be sought after. He wants to be sought after. He created you *for Himself*. You will only find completeness *when you find Him*. Scripture reminds us, "You will seek me and find me when you seek me with all your heart." (Jeremiah 29:13).

I was ten years old when my big brother led me to Jesus. He explained to me how we live in a broken world and how our brokenness separates us from God. He showed me that by praying and communicating with Jesus and asking Him to be the Lord of my life, I would be "born again" and my spirit would be restored back to God – and I'd get to walk through this life with Him. I accepted that and prayed the prayer, and my walk with the Lord Jesus began.

My big brother has always had an influence on me. He is ten years my senior and has loved and walked with God most of his life. When I was in junior high and high school, he was a youth pastor at a little non-denominational church in the middle of Kansas. Whenever I would visit him, I would get a taste of spiritual things that I didn't see anywhere else.

At my brother's church, they would often pray for sick people, and I would watch them get healed. I remember the church members praying for one man who had a leg shorter than the other, and I watched it physically grow out before my eyes. Another time I remember a demon-possessed boy being prayed for, and the demon speaking out of the boy's mouth to the pastors and fighting to come out. He was delivered, and such a peaceful change came over the boy afterwards. I saw passion and love for people from the church members and power from God that backed up their faith.

A childhood like this ruined me (in a good way) for Jesus forever. I got a taste for walking in what I believe we are supposed to be walking in (as Christians).

> As you go, proclaim this message: "The kingdom of heaven has come near." Heal the sick, raise the dead, cleanse those who have leprosy, drive out demons. Freely you have received; freely give. Matthew 10:7-8

This.

This is *the message* Jesus gave to his disciples.

In this passage, Jesus is telling the disciples to take this message first to the Jews, but later it is the message that is to be given to everyone. This. Is. The. Message. It is the shortest sermon ever. This is the good news: The Kingdom *has come*. He said later that we would do all of the things that Jesus did and even more. Jesus was Himself God, yet He chose to live with limitations as a man, so that we could follow in His footsteps. He is our example. We can walk as Jesus walked. In fact, He wants us to.

So that means the power and life of God in us should be leaking out of us. I don't want to seek after experiences for the sake of the experiences, but I want to see evidence of His power at work in my life as I trust and walk with Him in faith. I once heard a preacher say that miracles aren't the whole Gospel, but the Gospel is not whole without them.

My walk with Him has made my spiritual life so very exciting. It is, in fact, the most exciting part of my life. I love Him so much!

Do you know there are people who walk so closely with Him that He can translate them (move them from location to location) and use them to minister to people and it doesn't phase them? As in, one minute you are in your living room and the next minute in a hut in Africa, there to tell someone about Jesus. It's called translation, and I know more than one person who has experienced it. It's a little freaky, but it occurred in scripture (Acts 8:34-40), and it still occurs today.

Miracles from God also happen today. One first-hand miracle that I experienced impacted my faith deeply. In 2016, I had the opportunity to help feed African refugees at the border of Panama and Costa Rica, where there is a serious human trafficking problem. We had been regularly going to a specific refugee camp and were expecting 50-100 people that day. We only had enough food with us to feed about 100 people a 1-cup serving of chicken and rice. The grocer was out of cups, so the person in charge of bringing them bought plates instead. When we got there and set up to serve the food there was a lot of chaos. There were many more people than we had expected and the refugees started to rush us to get food.

6 6

The helpers quickly jumped in (before they were told to only give a 1-cup serving to each person) and started piling food onto the plates with 3-4 cups of food on each plate. With this much food on each plate, we would only be able to serve about 30 people.

Except we didn't serve 30 people. We served over 300. We continued to serve food until every last person was served a heaping plate of chicken and rice. We even had 6 plates of food left over. Everyone's bellies were filled in the name of Jesus, and we all glorified God as we realized He had multiplied the food just like He did with the fishes and the loaves in the Bible (John 6:1-14). This event was humbling and amazing and faith inspiring, even to the unbelievers who were helping serve with us. Serving and walking with God is not boring!

And while the spiritual realm seems to be activated with faith, there is a dark side I have seen manifest as well. I have traveled a bit and have seen demonic manifestations in Africa, but I have not experienced demonic activity as much in the U.S. I attribute that to intellectualism and overall disbelief in the supernatural in the U.S. But there is a man I know who evokes a demonic response wherever he is. He is a minister who walks deeply with God. He was with my brother for dinner in a popular chain restaurant in the U.S. The waitress refused to wait on them and looked at them angrily and physically hissed at him! He confided to my brother that this had happened before. Two other members of the wait staff cowered, had a sudden change in their demeanor, and hissed when the minister and my brother walked by. His relationship with Jesus evoked this demonic response.

I'm bringing up all of these stories to make you hunger for a deeper spiritual life. Don't feel badly if demons don't hiss at you! Don't strive to see miracles for miracles' sake. Instead, strive to know Him without borders. Don't put Him in a box. Strive to get to know the One who created you and knew you when you were yet in your mother's womb. *He is the only One who matters.* He is passionately longing after you, but you have to seek Him as well. (Jeremiah 29:13)

I want you to see that life with God is not boring and is not confined to the four walls of a church building. I'm not encouraging you seek out an "experience", but I want you to know that the depths of walking with our Savior include more than blind faith. He responds to us. He speaks. He. Is. Real. But learning to recognize Him and learning to hear His voice can take time, trust, and a heart that is actively seeking Him.

There isn't time for it all here, but 20 years of my journey includes learning how to hear God's voice. I wrote a book about it called *Snatchproof, The Art of Hearing God's Voice.* I mention it because I didn't grow up knowing that God speaks to us. I was never taught how to listen to hear His voice, but you can learn it. He speaks in many ways and you can learn how to hear Him, without feeling like you are crazy.

The longer you walk with Jesus in faith, the more you seek Him, and the more you trust Him, the more you will see evidence of His power at work in your life.

Our Father is our Heavenly Father who created the earth and all that is in it. We were intended to walk through life in relationship with Him, learning about the earth and His creation from Him... yet by Adam's one choice to gain knowledge without God's help, that original destiny was lost. Thankfully, Jesus restored us to the Father and to relationship with Him, and we can train ourselves to hear His voice and learn from Him again. The closer you get to Him, the deeper the rabbit hole goes...the more exciting and faith-filled life gets. When your hearts starts to burn for the things His heart burns for, you will find yourself in situations where He has opportunities to step in. When you take the risk to go feed hungry people, and you do everything you can in your power to feed them but come up short, He has an opportunity to step in and make up for your shortness with a miracle. When you start walking in His ways, you will experience His power as a side effect. *It will leak out of you.*

So what do you want out of life? How deep do you want to go with Him? What are you open to? Do you have Him in a box? Are you willing to allow the walls of your box fall down? Maybe it's time to embrace Him and trust that He is good and that His mercies endure forever. My encouragement is that you run after Him with passion. Search for Him. Seek Him. You will find Him. He wants to be found and promises to be found by you when you seek Him with all your heart.

Application

Answer in the spaces below the questions .

On a scale of 1 to 10, where would you say your faith in Jesus lies? _____

Do you believe He exists? _____

Do you believe in the Father and in the Holy Spirit?

_____

Do you believe He is good? _____

Do you believe He loves you specifically? _____

Do you believe that He *sees* you? _____

Are you afraid of intimacy with Him? If so, why? _____

_____

Are you ready to go with Him wherever He might take you? _____

Use these questions to begin formulating the vision statement for your spiritual life. Maybe you want to know Him intimately as never before. Maybe you want to hear His voice in your heart clearly. Perhaps you want to be in a partnership with Him to minister to people who need Him. Possibly, you want your faith to be increased. Maybe you want to be able to lay hands on the sick and see them recover. Formulate a few sentences to describe what you want for your spiritual life during the next few years, and then write it out as your Spiritual Vision Statement in the space on the next page.

Write your Spiritual Vision statement here :

_____

_____

_____

_____

_____

_____

_____

STEP 3: Journal and Pray

As you start to think about vision for your spiritual life and your walk with God, let's start with a prayer to bring His plan into focus.

"Dear Jesus, I want more of You. Take me deeper in our relationship. Take me higher than I've ever been. Hold my hand. Walk with me. Counsel me. Speak to me. Help me to hear Your voice and gain confidence in knowing that I hear You! In Jesus' name, amen."

To end today's study, let's do a journaling exercise. Write a letter to yourself from God. Do not worry if it feels silly at first. Just start writing from the perspective of God and have faith that His Spirit is in you and can guide your thoughts. Let it flow, and don't worry about how crazy it seems. Nobody has to read it but you, and God doesn't mind if you make mistakes. He loves that you want to learn to communicate and hear His voice. He is faithful and will be with you in this exercise. Often just by starting to write you are priming the pump for thoughts to start flowing. Start like this:

My child, I love you so much! I am so excited that you are seeking Me. I want to guide you and help you in this process of finding your vision. Let's talk about

_____

_____

_____

_____

_____

_____

_____

_____

_____

_____

_____

_____

_____

_____

_____

_____

_____

Vision for Your Emotional Health

WEEK 2
DAY 4

Psalm 37:4-5 (NKJV)
"Delight yourself also in the Lord, And He shall give
you the desires of your heart. Commit your way to the
Lord, Trust also in Him, And He shall bring it to pass."

STEP 1: Meditating on God's Word With Aromatherapy

Today we are going to try something new. You can still enjoy your essential oil by diffusing it if you have a diffuser. If you don't, put a few drops on the skin below both nostrils and breathe in the aroma. Now say the scripture *out loud* 4 times. Then say it to yourself inwardly 4 times. Then, see if you can repeat it once by memory. Next we will explore how to apply essential oils using the Vita Flex technique. Vita Flex is a specific technique that uses the touch of a person's fingers and nails to create an electric current through the body. When we use this technique on the foot, we often look at a common reflexology chart like the one on the next page:

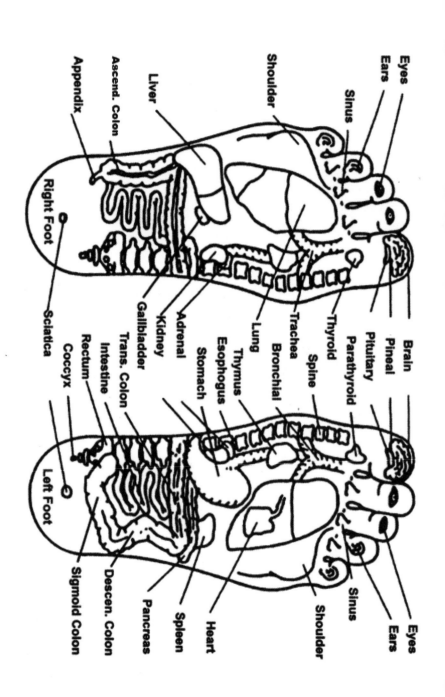

Essential oils travel along our nerve pathways, and since all of our nerves end in our feet, the reflexology chart helps us see where the nerve pathways terminate. The bottom of the big toe correlates to the brain. If you put your oil on that spot using the Vita Flex technique, it will travel through your nervous system to your brain.

Let's try the technique on your left foot. Remove your socks, and sit so that you can reach your foot. Apply a drop of oil to the bottom of your big toe. Rest your right hand fingers flat on the bottom of the big toe of your left foot. Roll your fingers up onto the fingertips and continue over onto your nails, using medium pressure. Slide your hand up the toe about ½-inch, and repeat this rolling-and-release motion over the entire big toe. Repeat this motion 3 times on both feet. For more guidance, visit the *Vision* page on HolyScents.org for a video of this technique, or you can search and find the technique elsewhere online.

Now we will apply essential oil to the Reflexology points of the second brain of the body known as the "belly." Scientists often refer to our gut as a "second brain." Our guts are embedded with around 100 million nerves, and there is evidence that our brains and guts communicate with each other. Our guts are sensitive to our emotions. For example, something can be "gut wrenching," or we can experience "butterflies" in our stomach. So today as we focus on emotions, let's perform the Vita Flex technique on the reflexology point for the gut too.

The Reflexology point for the gut is found on the bottom of the feet just above the heels. Apply the oil to this place using the Vita Flex technique as described above. This helps prepare our bodies for the topic of emotions that we are covering today.

These 2 "brains" are thought to communicate with each other as we process our emotions. By applying oils to the specific places on our feet, we are sending the oils to the corresponding places in our bodies to stimulate them and help them connect.

STEP 2: Read and Respond

An Emotionally Healthy Vision

BY YVONNE PACE & WENDY SELVIG

Whenever our physical body is sick, we pay close attention to it. If we have a fever, we bundle up and eat chicken soup. If we scrape an elbow, we add essential oils or ointment. We know how to take care of ourselves when our physical body is not well, but do we know how to tend to our psychological well-being?

How is your emotional health? Do you work hard to "keep it together" on the outside while struggling on the inside? We all struggle at times; that is the mark of being human. Maybe it is time for an emotional checkup to see where you have room for improvement. Here is the good news: Emotional health is attainable, and the Holy Spirit can help us with our emotions when we need it.

Our emotions have a purpose. They are like a compass that helps us navigate our lives. But sometimes compasses break and point us in the wrong direction. Strong emotions can encourage us to take action, but sometimes they are misguided and encourage us to take wrong actions. Emotions like fear, anger and guilt can often create untrue realities. When we believe the lies created by these emotions, we have allowed the enemy to deceive us. We have to check our emotional health every once in awhile to make sure we aren't being controlled by our emotions.

One way to check on your emotional health is to gauge how you handle stressful situations. For example, how do you handle unfair criticism when someone says something that you disagree with? Do you choose to react to the negative situation in a life-giving way, or do you respond by "letting them have it?"

It's easy to fly off the handle when we aren't in control of our emotions. Anger can flare up and a sense of justice can take over, causing you to want to be the enforcer of that justice. Deep wounds can make you want to protect yourself from any similar causes of pain. But when your wounds are healed, you can see beyond protecting your own heart. You can actually see the pain of the one who just criticized or spoke harshly to you. When someone slings his or her baggage at you, it's wonderful to be able to respond with love.

Nobody is perfect, and you can't always be ready for these opportunities. Most of the time they come unexpectedly. But you can prepare your heart and decide ahead of time how you will respond when this happens. You can receive healing for your wounds. *If you regularly "fly off the handle" and respond emotionally in stressful situations, that is an indication that your emotions may need a tune-up.*

How can we tune our emotions so that we don't respond poorly to stressful situations? Begin by identifying your "hot buttons" and triggers. We all have triggers that can set us up for failure in certain situations. What is a trigger? It is something that seems to create an automatic response from you. It can be an event, feeling, circumstance, or anything else that causes a specific reaction. When a trigger is activated, you typically respond quickly and without much thought, but still that reaction is a choice. Knowing how to identify your triggers can help you learn how to control your response to them.

What are your triggers? Do you know? Ask the Holy Spirit to reveal your triggers to you. To what do you typically react strongly? Are you told that there certain things to which you are sensitive? What makes you angry? What makes you insecure? These are your triggers.

Write down a few things that might be triggers for you. A few examples might be: being criticized, being alone, being rejected, being threatened, etc.

My Triggers

1. _____

2. _____

3. _____

Now search through the Word and find scriptures that can help you overcome these triggers. For example, maybe criticism is on your list of triggers. This is a common one for many people. When someone criticizes you, you may feel like it is an attack and immediately respond with anger. You can find scriptures that support your true identity so that you can agree with Christ and not take critical words from other people so personally. Here are a few examples of scriptures (and summaries of what they are about) that you can meditate on if criticism is your trigger:

I am born of God, and the evil one does not touch me. (1 John 5:18)

I am holy and without blame before Him in love. (Ephesians 1:4; 1 Peter 1:16)

I have the peace of God that passes all understanding. (Philippians 4:7)

I have received the gift of righteousness and reign as a king in life by Jesus Christ. (Romans 5:17)

I am God's workmanship, created in Christ unto good works. (Ephesians 2:10)

I am an overcomer by the blood of the Lamb and the word of my testimony. (Revelation 12:11)

When you apply your faith and prayer and renew your mind through scriptures, you can be freed from your triggers and negative emotions. This is the beginning of a decision to walk in the emotional health the Lord has called you to walk in as you serve Him.

Will you say the right thing every time? Probably not. Can you work on it and improve your reaction to people? You bet. If you sense that you have deep emotional wounds that need to be healed, please consider seeking help. There are several ways you can do this. You can seek out a licensed professional Christian counselor who can help you heal emotional wounds. There is nothing wrong with doing this, and seriously, everyone could benefit from some sessions with a good counselor! Another option is to find someone who is trained in Emotional Release. This is a Holy Spirit-led prayer healing technique that uses essential oils to stimulate your emotional (limbic) brain while you and the leader pray and ask the Holy Spirit to reveal things that need to be healed in your life. You go through a process of praying for and releasing those wounds. Make sure the person is CARE Certified to assist you with this process. You can find a directory of CARE Certified instructors at RaindropTraining.com.

Dear brothers and sisters, when troubles of any kind come your way, consider it an opportunity for great joy.
James 1:2 (NLT)

We need to have a different perspective on the stresses of this life, as they are opportunities to experience great joy. This joy comes from being led by the Spirit of God that dwells within us and from responding to emotionally challenging situations with grace and compassion towards those who lash out. This comes from being in a place where our own emotions are healed and we don't take stressful situations personally. Only then are we able to minister to and see the hurts of others effectively. Whew! That may be a big goal, but it is a great one to put on your vision board!

Application

Make a list of life-giving responses to your triggers. How can you respond in a life-giving way the next time your trigger is activated ?

_____

_____

_____

Now bring your thoughts together into a personal vision statement for your own emotional health and write it in the space below. To help guide you, consider these questions:

What would you like to see for yourself and your own mental health over the next year?

Do you need to pursue help for healing emotional wounds?

What are your action steps and your plan to receive help?

How would you like to be able to respond to triggers in your life?

Now write a vision statement for your own emotional health. What do you need to do, and where would you like to be in the future in regard to your emotional health?

_____

_____

_____

_____

Further Questions:

Do you need to forgive someone in your life and be able to go to the person and pray with him or her? If that isn't possible, do you just need to forgive someone?

Is the Holy Spirit leading you to study the technique of Emotional Release that we discussed earlier? Talk to your Bible study leader to see if they know someone who is trained in Emotional Release.

Step 3: Journal and Prayer

Write down a summary of the thoughts and emotions that have risen to the surface during this section of the study on your vision for emotional health. What emotions are unhealthy in your life? What needs healing?

_____

_____

_____

_____

_____

_____

End today by journaling and talking to the Lord about your triggers. Ask Him to heal those wounded areas in your life and to help you respond with life when these hot spots are triggered.

Week 2 Review & Meditation

WEEK 2
DAY 5

Congratulations for making it half way through the *Vision* aromatherapy Bible study! When you reach the end of the study, you will assemble the components of your vision onto your vision board. Don't forget to gather your materials for that final day – a corkboard, a poster board or even paper will do.

STEP 1: Meditating on God's Word with Aromatherapy

Today is a day of review. Allow yourself space to think and reflect over what you have learned the past week. Use your chosen method to inhale your oil blend for a few minutes before you complete today's lesson. Calm your mind. Get into a relaxed state and reflect on the weekly scripture. Were you able to memorize it?

Review your thoughts and prayers and see if you can remember the scripture for the week without looking. Write it out here:

STEP 2: Writing Down Your Vision

The review boxes for this week on the following pages will provide details for you to include on your vision board. Write down answers to the following:

1. Review your thoughts about having a vision for your family. Write your vision for your family in the box below:

My Vision For My Family:

2. What is a gift or passion God has given you that you would exercise even if you never got paid for it? What is your dream vocation? If you don't have a specific job in mind, what elements would make up a dream vocation (i.e. travel, working with people, etc.)?

My Vision For My Vocation:

3. Review what you wrote in the section about spiritual vision. Where do your want your relationship with God to go? Write your spiritual vision in the box below:

My Spiritual Vision:

4. Based on the answers you gave during the lesson, what is your emotional vision for yourself?

My Emotional Vision:

While still diffusing and breathing in your oil blend, write out a prayer that engages the Father about these issues. Commit your ways in these areas to Him.

Vision For Your Health

WEEK 3
DAY 1

Jeremiah 29:11
"For I know the plans I have for you, declares
the Lord, plans to prosper you and not to harm
you, plans to give you hope and a future."

STEP 1: Meditating on God's Word With Aromatherapy

Today we will review and expand more on the Vita Flex Technique. Vita Flex literally means "vitality of the reflexes." The Vita Flex technique is believed to have come from ancient Tibet. When we combine essential oil application and Vita Flex Technique, it is even more powerful.

Our bodies have intricate electrical pathways. We have many nerves in our feet, and since essential oils like to travel along nerve pathways, our feet are a good place to put the oils. The Vita Flex technique produces an electrical charge (caused by the fingers contacting skin) and uses the body's reflexes to transmit the therapeutic effects of essential oils into the body. There are places on your feet that correlate to systems and organs of your body. When you apply oils to those specific places using the Vita Flex technique, you are doing double duty: your fingers are sending an electrical charge up the nerve pathway, and the essential oils are traveling along those pathways to the desired place, supporting that area of your body.

Let's try it again today!

1. First, apply your oil or oil blend to one of your bare feet. Use your right hand to apply to your left foot, and vice-versa. Start by applying the oil along the inside arch of your foot. This is the area associated with your spine.

2. Now apply the Vita Flex technique with your fingers. Place the fleshy part, or pads, of your fingertips along the arch of your foot. Using a quick, rolling motion, roll your fingers forward so that first your fingertips, and then your fingernails, come in contact with your foot. Beginning at the heel, use this rolling motion up the length of your arch.

When your fingers touch your foot, an electrical charge is created. As you roll your fingers and the nail touches the skin, it interrupts the charge and sends little electrical charges, along with the essential oils, down the pathways.

Try it on both feet! By applying the oils to your feet and using the Vita Flex method, you will send the oil into your body quickly.

After applying your oil, spend 3-5 minutes meditating on the verse for this week, Jeremiah 29:11.

Step 2: Read and Respond

Apply 2 drops of your oil or oil blend to your wrists, and/ or continue to diffuse or inhale the scent as you read this next section.

Vision For Your Health
We Belong to Him - Spirit, Soul and Body!

BY YVONNE PACE

What do you really desire for your physical body? Long life? No disease? Strong muscles? Weight loss? Let's spend some time renewing our minds in the Word of God so that you can get His perspective and vision for your physical body.

I Corinthians 6:19-20 states that our body is a temple where the Holy Spirit lives. The scriptures go on to say that we don't own ourselves and that God paid a very high price to make us His, therefore we are to honor God with our bodies. We have the choice each day to follow either our flesh/sinful nature or the born again spirit that was provided for us by Jesus' death on the cross!

*So letting your sinful nature control your mind
leads to death, but letting the Spirit of God
control your mind leads to life and peace.
Romans 8:6*

We have to make decisions to eat healthy, exercise and honor God with what we put in our bodies. Our sinful nature is selfish and self-pleasing. It desires things that make the body feel good temporarily, but ultimately harms or brings death. Choosing to put good things in our bodies is a choice we make that honors God with our bodies.

Nobody is perfect when it comes to keeping his or her body healthy and pure, but there are some core decisions we can make to improve our health and to honor the temple of the Holy Spirit that we have been given.

Consider the following as you decide what you want for your own health and the vision you create for your body:

1. Fuel your body with the things God made. He is really smart. He put enzymes, vitamins, minerals, and so much more into the fruits and vegetables that grow in the earth. Our bodies need an adequate supply of these foods to repair cells and to give us energy.

2. Consider eating non-GMO and organic foods whenever it is possible. The non-GMO carrots cost a dollar more? Cut back on something else to make it happen so that you can properly energize your body without causing harm. The dollar you spend now might save you thousands later by helping you avoid long-term illness down the road.

3. Remove the toxic chemicals from your home and life. There are thousands and thousands of chemicals used in our foods and cleaning products that have never been tested for safety! They are known carcinogens, and yet we somehow think that if they are sold on the grocery store shelves and "everyone uses them," they are safe. Ask yourself why 1 out of 3 people in the U.S. will be afflicted with cancer in their lifetime. Find products that are chemical-free to replace the ones that are not.

4. Use unadulterated essential oils from Young Living to support the systems of your body. Do not buy essential oils at a grocery store or at large retailers. We do not know of one brand sold in those markets that is safe. Oils support body systems. There are oils that can help your respiratory system, circulatory system, excretory system, etc. There are oils that specifically support the heart, liver, kidneys, skin, etc. When you have weaknesses in these areas, you can apply the oil that supports that system or body part and let your body use it's incredible immune system to heal itself.

5. "A sedentary lifestyle is the new 'smoking'." I heard this recently and chuckled, but it is true. The more we are moving and the more we exercise, the better we feel. But it is often too easy to not get moving. Consider adding a daily walk into your lifestyle, or if you are more active or capable, challenge yourself by moving a lot more.

6. Research GMO wheat and how genetically modified wheat has more chromosomes and genomes than it should – and how the human body doesn't know what to do with it. Genetically modified wheat could be the key to many health problems today. Here are a few resources I recommend on this topic: *Ancient Einkorn, Today's Staff of Life* by D. Gary Young; *Wheat Belly*, by Dr. William Davis MD; *Grain Brain*, by Dr. David Perlmutter. These authors and health care providers give practical instructions and recipes to get you started on taking control of your health. These changes can help you gain the strength and stamina needed to honor the Lord with the physical body that He has given you with which to serve Him while living on the earth.

Application

We want to help you identify a goal for your body. Only you know where you are now and where you want to be. Your goal may be to achieve a healthy weight, to eat healthier, become more active, or anything else regarding your health. Write three goals you'd like to achieve in the next year regarding your body:

1. _____

2. _____

3. _____

STEP 3: Journal and Pray

Prayerfully ask the Lord what your health focus should be. What does He have to say about your body? What does He want to see happen for your health and well-being? Not sure? Ask! And then listen. Get quiet and write yourself a letter from God and see if the Holy Spirit speaks to you through your writing. Don't worry if this exercise feels silly; nobody has to read it but you.

_____

_____

_____

_____

_____

_____

_____

_____

_____

End with prayer: Write your prayer to the Lord asking for His wisdom for how to honor Him with your body:

_____

_____

_____

_____

_____

_____

Vision For Fun

WEEK 3
DAY 2

Jeremiah 29:11
"For I know the plans I have for you, declares
the Lord, plans to prosper you and not to harm
you, plans to give you hope and a future."

STEP 1: Meditating on God's Word With Aromatherapy

Diffuse your oil as you are meditating on the above scripture. Apply a drop under your nose and to the inside of each wrist. If you so desire, use the Vita Flex method you used yesterday to apply your essential oil to your feet.

Spend a minimum of 3 to 5 minutes breathing the scent and reading the scripture. (You can spend much longer if you choose to.) Allow yourself to think about one part of this scripture at a time. Does God really want to prosper you? Does He want to keep you from harm? Does He care if you have fun sometimes and enjoy life? If the answer isn't yes, ask yourself where you get that belief.

STEP 2: Read and Respond

Make sure you continue to breathe the scent as you are reading.

Vision For Fun

BY WENDY SELVIG

*"Also that everyone should eat and drink and take
pleasure in all his toil – this is God's gift to man."*
Ecclesiastes 3:13 (ESV)

What is "fun" to you? Some people can answer this
question right away, because they live for fun! Others have
a difficult time even defining the word because they think
they don't have time for it. You may be wondering why
we are including the category of "fun" in the vision for our
lives? As human beings, we need to have some fun, and if
we think about it and make plans, we can have memorable
experiences that bring joy to our lives. Sometimes we just
need to plan to have fun.

Also, we are responsible for the memories made for our
children. The world can be a difficult place and life can be
tough, so it is wonderful when we can plan some fun for
our families to enjoy and create memories together.

Okay, so put on your thinking cap and pretend you own
the cattle on a thousand hills. (Oh wait, your Heavenly
Father does!) If resources were unlimited, or at least not
that limited, where would you go and what would you do
for fun?

If you have children, your idea might be completely
different than if you don't. I have a few ideas for my "fun"
vision. I have three boys, and I want to take them all to
Disney World. This is not going to be a cheap vacation.
But it would be so much fun. My kids would never forget
it, and so it is on my vision board. It is going to take some
planning, dreaming, saving, and a little help from Father
God. But there is a better chance of it happening when it is

on my vision board. I've written down my vision, and it is before me every day. My subconscious works to make it happen and heralds can run with the vision (Habakkuk 2:2).

Enough about my vision...what is yours? You only get one life to live, and there is an entire world of opportunity out there. What do you want to do for fun in this life?

Application

Answer the questions below.

1. SMALL FUN: Are you good at having fun or do you need to plan for it? Think about the next year. What is something you can plan to do that doesn't cost a lot of money? Maybe an evening out with a girlfriend for coffee and a movie? What about taking your family to spend the night at a hotel and go swimming there? (Kids think hotels are so fun!) What about individual fun dates with your children? You may relish the idea of an afternoon away from everyone just to shop or even sit at a library alone. Whatever sounds fun to you – on the low-cost scale – write it in the space below:

_____

_____

_____

_____

Now, get the calendar out and get to planning. Write in some dates, and call friends if you need to. Make a date for fun, and follow through to make it happen!

2. BIG FUN: What sounds fun to you that might cost more money than you have? For example, it might take time to save up money to go on a trip. If you had

9 5

two to five years to plan for a major trip and were able to save money towards that trip every month, where would you go? Choose one place that you'd like to go the most, and write it down in the space below. Your trip might be with your significant other, a good friend, or your children. What would make a lasting memory? What kind of trip would be worth talking about for years to come? Choose one place and write it in the space below. If a trip doesn't sound like fun, what does? Write about that instead.

Is money pretty tight? Have you thought about finding something you can do on the side to make money for your trip? Do you bake good cookies? Can you sew for people? Walk dogs? Share essential oils? Did you know that every time you help someone get a Young Living membership with a Premium Starter Kit, Young Living sends you a check for $50? Ask your Bible Study leader for details.

Whatever your avenue for extra income, devise a plan to make it happen. Extra work now can mean an extra fun time later. You'll have the memory and the satisfaction that you worked hard to make the idea into reality for life.

Step 3: Journal and Pray

As you start to think about your vision for the area of fun, start with a prayer to bring His plan into focus. You can use this prayer or craft your own.

"Heavenly Father, thank You for creating me with the capacity to have pleasure. I want to honor You even in what I do for fun. I ask for Your help as I try to be intentional with my fun activities. Thank You for putting desires in my heart. Now guide and direct me as I make plans for my life. Help me with my plans and show me ways to pay for the plans. Help me to create wonderful, fun memories for my family and friends and allow this vision to be a blessing in someone's life down the road. In Jesus' name, amen."

Vision For Your Finances

WEEK 3
DAY 3

Jeremiah 29:11
"For I know the plans I have for you, declares
the Lord, plans to prosper you and not to harm
you, plans to give you hope and a future."

STEP 1: Meditating on God's Word With Aromatherapy

Today we are going to show you a "neurological" way to meditate on the scripture. It has been proven through MRI that by performing this process with anything that you want to remember, your brain will connect new dendrites (part of the communication network system of the brain involved in memory) in your brain.

While you are enjoying your essential oil today, say a portion of this week's scripture <u>out loud</u> 4 times. Before you lie down to sleep tonight, say the same portion of scripture <u>out loud</u> by reading it 4 times again. Inhale your essential oil. Lie down and without moving, try to repeat the same portion of scripture <u>in your mind</u>. If you get stuck, you may read it out loud again. If you can remember the scripture, fall asleep meditating on that portion of the verse.

Step 2: Read and Respond

Apply 2 drops of the oil blend to your wrists, and/or continue to diffuse or inhale the scent as you read this next section. Make sure you breathe the scent as you are reading.

Are You Hopeful About Your Financial Future?

BY YVONNE PACE

Our meditation scripture this week assures us that God knows the plans that He has for our lives. It continues further to say that our future does not need to be a disaster, but rather it can be full of goodness and hope.

Let's look at the context of this scripture. King Nebuchadnezzar exiled the children of Israel to Babylon. While in exile, the Israelites received a letter from the prophet Jeremiah that said they would be exiled for 70 years in Babylon, and then God would allow them to return back home to Jerusalem. Their journey home included an important requirement. The scripture says in verse 12 that *if they seek God with their whole heart,* He would restore them and they would return to Jerusalem. That scripture also says this included restoring their fortunes, or in today's vernacular, their finances. Do your finances need help? Do they need to be restored?

> *Seek the Kingdom of God above all else, and*
> *He will give you everything you need.*
> *Luke 12:31 (NLT)*

100

This verse speaks of our priorities and again, our hearts. So in order to get to a place where we want to submit our finances to God and have a vision of hope in this area for the future, our hearts must belong to Him and we must be seeking the Kingdom of God.

Can I ask you a difficult question? How do you handle comparison? Do you often compare yourself to your friends and family? Do you wish you could upsize to a bigger house? Are your clothes not good enough, or you feel you need more? Whether your finances are in terrific shape or in need of a miraculous restoration from God, there is one thing we all need to settle in our hearts as we try to better ourselves financially. That is to learn how to find *contentment*. It doesn't matter if you own the biggest mansion in town, if you don't learn the art of contentment, it still won't be enough. You can live on a dirt floor in the hills and still learn to be content. Contentment is a powerful thing that can help you throughout your life, whether you are in a phase where you have money or not. Now look at the following verse that addresses contentment:

> *But godliness actually is a means of great gain when accompanied by contentment. For we have brought nothing into the world, so we cannot take anything out of it either. If we have food and covering, with these we shall be content.*
> *I Timothy 6:6-8 (NASB)*

Stuff is just *stuff*. Houses can be big and fancy or they can be small, but it's the people inside that make the home. If your house isn't as nice as your neighbor's, who cares? While we learn to move forward and get out of debt, we can find contentment in each stage we are in – whether that is "less wealthy" or "more."

Being content doesn't mean that you should not have goals; it just means that you do not panic about your current situation and you realize that you don't always have to have that next-best thing. As long as you have food and shelter, you should be content. It's okay to live in a little cheap apartment to save money so that you can get out of debt tomorrow. There is contentment for that.

Can you image what it was like for the Israelites to try to be content while waiting 70 years to be able to go back home and to have their financial position in life restored!? Hopefully it won't take you 70 years to recover your finances, but even if it does, you can be content in the process if you don't allow "stuff" to have a hold on you. *Stuff* is not your master, and you can be content when you have covering and food because you don't get to take it with you when you die anyway.

That being said, contentment is not a license to be irresponsible with your money either. If you have money and are a good steward, you can impact the Kingdom of God and help people much more than if you have none. You get one life; how are you going to live it? If you need help in this area, find the best teacher and learn. Go see a financial adviser. Seek out the financial guru section of your nearest bookstore and get a book or two that might help you in this area. It is a godly thing to have your finances in order. And when you really master money, you can provide things, like education and businesses, for your children and your grandchildren.

A good man leaves an inheritance for his children's children.
Proverbs 13:22 (KJV)

It is a good thing to have your finances in order and to honor God with your money. May we all find contentment where we are (not always wanting better houses, cars, etc.) and get the help we need to get ahead and master our money.

Application

Answer the questions below.

What are your strengths when it comes to your finances?

_____

_____

_____

What are your weaknesses when it comes to your finances?

_____

_____

_____

Remember in the book of Jeremiah where God said the Israelites needed to seek Him with their whole hearts? What does that mean, to seek the Lord with our whole heart?

_____

_____

_____

Do you need to learn to be content with what you have?

_____

_____

Do you have shelter and food?

_____

_____

If you have your debt under control and your finances are in order, what can you do to "leave an inheritance for your children's children?"

_____

_____

_____

_____

Do you struggle with saving consistently? Remember your fun vision? Do you need to find a strategy to discipline yourself so that you have the finances to be able to fulfill this vision?

_____

_____

These questions are here to guide you as you develop your financial vision statement. What needs to happen with your finances over the next year? Do you need to seek help? Do you need to carve out time to get organized? Do you want to start tithing more and honoring God with your finances? Do you need to study the scriptures to discover more about what God has said regarding your finances? Pick out several things you want to accomplish and see in your finances over the next year or so, and *write them down* in the space below as your financial vision statement.

_____

_____

_____

_____

_____

STEP 3: Journal and Pray

Write down your prayer here, keeping in mind that the Lord Jesus has given you the authority to walk through this life by the power of the Holy Spirit. You do have a hope for a strong financial future. Don't let discouragement cloud your hopes for honoring the Lord with your wealth! May the Lord bless you as your faith becomes stronger and the Lord leads you to the next step toward achieving your financial goals. Remember whom you are in Christ and that you can do all things by the power of the resurrection, amen. (So be it!)

106

Vision For Your Relationships

WEEK 3
DAY 4

Psalm 37:4-5
"Delight thyself also in the LORD; and he shall give thee the desires of thine heart. Commit thy way unto the LORD; trust also in him; and he shall bring it to pass."

STEP 1: Meditating on God's Word With Aromatherapy

Diffuse your oil as desired, and spend 5 minutes breathing in the aroma and thinking about the scripture.
By the end of this week, we hope that you will know this scripture by heart and you will have thoroughly dissected it and have deep thoughts about it. Allow this time to be special. Allow your mind to rest and soak in the scent and thoughts about the scripture.

Step 2: Read and Respond

Apply 2 fresh drops of the oil blend to your wrists, and/or continue to diffuse or inhale the scent as you read this next section.

Your Relationship Vision

BY WENDY SELVIG

Dads and moms, husbands and wives, brothers and sisters, children, cousins, friends and business associates: these are all important relationships that we need to get "right" in our lives. Yet relationships can be tricky. The problem is that they involve people, and people are often broken and always imperfect.

When Adam and Eve chose to eat of the tree of the knowledge of good and evil, they made a choice to live life without God's help. They broke their relationship with Him and therefore broke the relationship between God and the entire human race. Before they took fruit from that tree, they had been learning about life directly from their walks with Father God in the Garden of Eden. It was a mentorship as well as a Father/child relationship. It was good. They would walk through the garden together, and the couple would get their wisdom from the Father... and as the scripture tells us, IT WAS GOOD. But then the serpent came and tempted them. He caused them to doubt God's goodness and suggested that they learn and get wisdom on their own, without Him. That was the choice that separated them from God and set the empty path that all mankind has been on ever since. Now, without God, the human race gets to figure out life without the insight from the One who created it all.

The tree that Adam and Eve partook of is said to contain the knowledge of good and evil. What is evil? It is the absence of God. So they were gaining "knowledge" both from God (good) and without God (evil). The choice to take this fruit, was a choice to gain wisdom outside of their relationship with God. They were going to learn on their own, without Him.

This set up the entire human race for failure because it separated us from walking through life in a relationship with God. We come into the world broken and without relationship with Him. It is only after we accept His peace offering, the sacrifice of His Son Jesus, and we choose to come into relationship with Him again that our position with God is made right. Life is restored in Him. It's the way He designed it to be.

Understanding this is foundational to having right relationships with everyone else in our lives. We first have to make right our relationship with God. That can be done with a simple prayer of recognition that we are broken without knowing Him. Ask Him to come into your life and to fellowship with you. Scripture says He will seal you with the Holy Spirit. Then rest in the fact that He will walk with you and counsel you and love on you the rest of your days! Spending time reading the Bible, praying and journaling will help you to develop an ear for hearing His voice in your daily walk. Once you have the counsel of the Holy Spirit within you, He will help you figure out the other relationships in your life.

Your family relationships are unique to you. If you are married, your spouse is nobody else's spouse. The child you have together is nobody else's child. The parents and siblings you have are uniquely yours. Our family relationships are very specific to us and are often the most challenging!

A friend loves at all times, and a brother is born for adversity.
Proverbs 17:17 (KJV)

The set of people we are placed with is our family and our unique challenge. They are the ones to whom we get to learn to show love and patience throughout our entire lives, as we are likely to have some relationships with differing personalities and opinions.

Though we are stuck with family members for better or worse, we do get to choose our spouses and friends. Our dating relationships and spouse relationships are very important, as are intimate friendships. We should choose our close friends wisely. We have to guard our hearts and our emotions from forming attachments in unhealthy relationships and with people who do not love and know God.

Guard your heart above all else, for it
determines the course of your life.
Proverbs 4:23 (NLT)

Don't team up with those who are unbelievers. How can
righteousness be a partner with wickedness? How can light live
with darkness? What harmony can there be between Christ and
the devil? How can a believer be a partner with an unbeliever?
2 Corinthians 6:14-15 (NLT)

These scriptures do not say that we can't have friends who are not believers, rather it warns us against being "yoked" with unbelievers. According to Miriam Webster, a yoke is a wooden bar or frame by which two draft animals (such as oxen) are joined at the heads or necks for working together. When oxen are yoked together, they move as one. To yoke is to walk intimately with; to go the same direction as; to bear a burden together. Believing in God and not believing in God are such polar opposite paths that it is impossible to be yoked and to be walking the two paths. One will take the other one with them, or the two will find themselves torn apart.

Yoking with an unbeliever causes great tearing and pain, or you just go nowhere. If two oxen want to move in different directions, the stronger one usually pulls the weaker one along in his direction, or they just stand still and accomplish nothing. You'd be better off to not be yoked at all than to be yoked with one who is going the opposite direction. Therefore, choose your mate and your intimate friends wisely.

Walk with the wise and become wise, for a companion of fools suffers harm.
Proverbs 13:20

Who are your close friends and confidants? What do you desire in your future in regard to your relationships? You may be single, desiring a God-loving mate. You may be unequally yoked, desiring for your mate to come to know God. You may be longing for a stronger relationship with a family member. You may want restoration in a broken relationship. Maybe you desire a good friend. Take some time to really ponder and think of your future and what you would like it to look like in regard to your relationships and write your desire in the space below:

If you are a Christian and are already married to an unbeliever, it may be the biggest challenge of your life. A few scriptures that may guide you: 1 Corinthians 7:12-14, Philippians 2:14, 1 Peter 3:1, and 1 Corinthians 7:17. Look for ways to glorify God through your circumstances and find faith support outside of your relationship through church or other believers.

_____

_____

_____

_____

_____

_____

_____

STEP 3: Journal and Pray

Now take the desire you have written and journal about it. What do you think you need to do to acquire what you want? How can you pray to help achieve your vision? Be honest and ask the Holy Spirit to enlighten you and help you walk the path towards the relationship vision you have for your near future.

_____

_____

_____

_____

_____

_____

_____

_____

_____

_____

End with Prayer:

"Lord I am excited and expectant about my future and the relationships You have given me. I am seeking You for help with all of my relationships. Please help me to heal in areas where I need healing so that I can be a good friend, a good spouse, a good parent, a good child, etc. I want to have God-honoring relationships, and I need Your help to do it. Please give me wisdom to make my relationships healthy and successful. I give You praise and thanks, In Jesus' name, amen."

(This is just a model prayer; you can change it and make it more applicable to your personal situation.)

Week 3 Review & Meditation

W E E K   3
D A Y   5

STEP 1: Meditating on God's Word With Aromatherapy

Today is a day of review. Start by making sure your diffuser is operating with your chosen oil or by inhaling the oil from your hands. As you breathe the scent, reflect over the things you have meditated on this past week in regard to vision.

Take 5 minutes to reflect on the weekly scripture.

Were you able to memorize it?

Jeremiah 29:11
"For I know the plans I have for you, declares
the Lord, plans to prosper you and not to harm
you, plans to give you hope and a future."

Take time to read through your notes from this week. Review your thoughts and prayers, and see if you can write out the scripture from memory in the space below:

_____

_____

_____

_____

_____

_____

STEP 2: Writing Down Your Vision

Write in the boxes the answers to the following:

1. What were the three goals you wrote for yourself in the chapter on having a vision for your health? Write them in the box below:

My Vision For Health:

2. What are the two fun things (a small fun and a big fun idea) you came up with in the vision for fun chapter? We asked you to think of an immediate, low-cost fun thing you could do and a longer-term, possible trip, you could take for fun. Write your two responses in the box below:

My Vision For Fun:

3. What is your vision for your personal finances? Write it in the box:

My Vision For Finances:

4. What do you desire in your future relationships? What did you write down about relationships this week? Write your answers in the box below:

My Vision For Relationships:

While still diffusing and breathing in your oil blend, write out a prayer that engages the Father about the issues we have covered this week. Commit these areas to Him and ask Him to help you to see them to be fulfilled. He loves you so much and I know He is more than willing to support you as you are seeking Him for help with these areas.

116

Who Am I? (Part 1)

W E E K   4
D A Y   1

Habakkuk 2:2 (ESV)
"And the LORD answered me: 'Write the vision; make
it plain on tablets, so he may run who reads it.'"

STEP 1: Meditating on God's Word
With Aromatherapy

Diffuse or inhale your oil as you meditate on the
above scripture.

When the Lord told Habakkuk to write down the vision,
He was answering the prophet's complaints from chapter
one about the Chaldeans. The Chaldeans were committing
all kinds of crimes against the Jewish nation, and
Habakkuk wanted to know if the Lord was going to help.
Jehovah answered with a vision of the future where the
Chaldeans are punished and the Jews are delivered, but He
also told him that the solution wasn't coming immediately.
Therefore, He wanted the vision... the good news... the
answer... to be written down, so that when it came to pass,
people would believe that God spoke to Habakkuk.

When we seek God for answers and direction, it is good to
write down the direction we receive. Just like Habakkuk,
we can write the vision on a tablet so that it is plain for us
to see on a daily basis to remind us of the direction and
the thoughts that came from Him. Then when the vision
comes to pass, we can believe that God spoke to us.

Spend another 3 to 5 minutes breathing your essential oil and reading this scripture. Allow yourself to think about parts of the scripture one at a time. Allow your mind to rest, and soak in the scent and the meaning of the scripture.

STEP 2: Read and Respond

Apply 2 drops of the oil blend to your wrists, and continue to diffuse or inhale the scent as you read this next section. Make sure you breathe the scent as you are reading.

The 25 Word Statement of Who You Are

BY WENDY SELVIG

Dr. Daniel Daves is an author, public speaker and financial advisor. He's also my big brother. What I'm about to share with you I have taken from him (with his permission). He actually doesn't mind me sharing it with you and didn't even ask for a plug for his book called *The Compass Guide* (available on Amazon). (But I'm a good sister and am sharing it with you anyway.)

This year, my entire family sat down with Daniel and he walked us through one of the chapters in his book. The chapter helps you define who you are and who God made you to be. I can't believe I went 44 years without actually defining this information in my own life. The exercise I am sharing with you today will help you to mine out of yourself the nuggets and jewels you often can't clearly see. My hope is that when you are finished, you will have a pile of jewels that come together and create a clearer picture of who you are and what is within you.

I'm going to explain the exercise to you, and it may look like this day's work is the shortest exercise yet. Don't let the amount of ink on the page fool you; this exercise might take you the longest. You are going to craft a sentence that completely spells out who you are. This could take days, even weeks if you choose to allow it. Just promise yourself that you will complete a version of it today and tomorrow. It will serve you well to finish it and have it on your vision board. Do whatever it takes to construct your sentence, even if you have to go back and refine it later.

Application

Start thinking of words that describe you. This is not always easy to do. I will give you some examples to help you get started. Your assignment is to write 40-50 words that describe yourself on the next few pages. You will whittle them down later, so just write what comes to mind for now. Think big. If you're a dreamer and you tend to think in the "big picture" realm with new ideas all the time, write down "visionary". It's okay to think big for yourself with this exercise. Here are some examples from other people's statements:

Mother, wife, husband, father, trainer, leader, peaceful, prophetic, apostolic, CEO, people-person, follower, deep, decisive, team-player, Spirit-led, friend, visionary, thoughtful, writer, cat-lover, dog-lover, healer, medic, doctor, punctual, popular, patient, hopeful, joyful, time-conscious, organized, respectful, sweet, thoughtful, teacher, shepherd, pastor, singer, worshiper, worship-leader, supportive, strong, passionate, calm, orderly, helpful, natural-health-promoter, Bible-lover, football-lover, attentive, compassionate, mercy-giver, wound-binder, prayer-warrior, runner, lover, artist, protector, wall-destroyer, fighter, producer, warrior, counselor.

As you come up with 40-50 words that describe you, think of your personality traits. Think of your profession or training. Think of your hobbies. Think of your leadership skills. Think of your family roles. Think of the things deep in your spirit, yearnings unfulfilled.

Think of the global vision statement, the local community statement, and the individual areas we have taken you through. Does anything stand out about your comments that can help you describe yourself? What are your positive traits? Begin to gather words on the next few pages until you have 40-50. We will craft the sentence tomorrow. Good luck!

_____

_____

_____

_____

_____

_____

_____

_____

_____

End with Prayer:
"Heavenly Father, thank you for this opportunity to help me see who You have created me to be. Bring to my mind words that describe who I am. Holy Spirit please speak to my heart as I come up with these positive words that describe what You have made me to be. I commit this process to You, in Jesus' name, amen."

(This is just a model prayer, you can change it to make it more applicable to your personal situation.)

Who Am I? (Part 2)

WEEK 4
DAY 2

Habakkuk 2:2 (ESV)
"And the LORD answered me: 'Write the vision; make
it plain on tablets, so he may run who reads it.'"

STEP 1: Meditating on God's Word With Aromatherapy

Diffuse your oil as you are meditating on the above scripture. Put a few drops under your nose and on your wrist as you meditate on the scripture today. Recall from our lesson yesterday that God told Habakkuk to write the good news of the vision down, so that heralds can run with it. He wanted it engraved on tables of wood so that it could be read over and over and understood plainly. This way, heralds could take the good news of God's answer and vision to everyone.

God's vision was set in the heavenly realms, and God knew what His answer and the outcome were going to be. Habakkuk did not. To get the answer from heaven to earth, Habakkuk had to write the vision down while on earth.

Who are the heralds in your life? Who might possibly run with your vision if they saw it written down? The first person who will run with the vision is YOU. When your vision is put on paper in front of your eyes, your subconscious goes to work to help you make it happen. The Holy Spirit can cooperate with you to help make it

121

happen. Even angels, who work behind the scenes, can see it and might help to make it happen. Bring the vision of God for your life from the heavenly realm into the earthly realm by <u>writing it down</u>.

Allow this time to be special. Slow down. Allow your mind to rest and soak in the scent of the essential oil and ponder what the scripture means to you.

Step 2: Read and Respond

Continue to breathe the scent of the essential oil as you work through this section.

25 Word Statement - Part 2

BY WENDY SELVIG

Go to yesterday's exercise and look at the list of 40-50 words that you wrote to describe yourself. If you don't have 40-50 words yet, take some time to finish that right now. From that list, choose the best 25 words that you wrote. Circle the words you want to keep, cross out the ones that are of minor importance. Do this until you feel that you have the 25 words that best describe you. Then put them together to craft a sentence. Here's the thing... the sentence doesn't have to be grammatically perfect! On the following page are a few samples from people who have done this exercise. Take note that their sentences aren't grammatically perfect, but they have used every word in the best way, and I can attest that the sentences really describe the people who wrote them!

Love, help and support for family, animals, the underdog, missions, and natural health. Faithful, confedant and friend, providing others needs. Passion for bookkeeping and accounting.

Using media ministry, music, leadership teams, and God given wealth to reach the nations for Christ. Learning languages, encouraging others, and training them to go.

MY 25 Word Statement

Kingdom Creator Producer Writer Leader Teacher Finance Generator Visionary Hears Loves God Prophet Warrior Worship Leader Healer Truth Seeker Problem Solver Family Caretaker Generous Friend

Application

Your job today is to craft your 25-word statement. It can only have 25 words, so make them count. You can use words like "to" and "and", but it is better if you can craft a sentence without them. Do your best to write a sentence that most describes you. Don't be surprised if this exercise takes a lot of time; you will find that it is well worth it to push through!

STEP 3: Journal and Pray

Use the journal space below to craft your sentence. When you are finished, write your 25-word statement in the box.

My Vision For Fun:

30 Days From Now

WEEK 4
DAY 3

Habakkuk 2:2 (ESV)
"And the LORD answered me: 'Write the vision; make it plain on tablets, so he may run who reads it.'"

STEP 1: Meditating on God's Word With Aromatherapy

Choose how you would like to apply your essential oil today. Diffuse, inhale from the bottle, put on your wrists, rub on the bottoms of your feet, or apply to the Vita Flex areas of your feet. You can use multiple application methods if you'd like. Spend 5 minutes reading and meditating on this scripture. Allow your mind to rest and soak in the aroma and the meaning of the scripture.

STEP 2: Read and Respond

Continue to breathe in your chosen oil. Make sure you breathe the scent as you are reading.

30 Days From Now

BY WENDY SELVIG

How are you feeling about your goals and your vision now? I really hope that you have some new insight about who you are and what your vision and purpose is. You might have hit a few mental blocks along the way. If you found yourself leaving some areas unfinished, go back today and revisit those areas. See if they are clearer after giving yourself a few days to ponder.

Now I want you to think of something you can do to further your vision in the next 30 days. Following is a list of the areas we have focused on. You can create action steps for all of them if you feel so inclined, but I suggest that you pick four specific areas and write something you can do to continue forward in each of them. For example, if your Relationship Vision involves spending more time with your children, taking steps to plan a special night out with them this month is a possible action step.

Circle 4 areas you want to create action steps for this month:

Global Vision	Emotional Vision
Local Vision	Health Vision
Family Vision	Fun Vision
Vocational Vision	Finances Vision
Spiritual Vision	Relationships Vision

Now write your action steps for those 4 areas below:

_____

_____

_____

_____

_____

_____

_____

Step 3: Journal and Pray

End your time today with a prayer of thankfulness to God for revealing who He has made you to be and for the vision of your life. Ask for help with walking out your vision with purpose and strength and dignity. Breathe your essential oil and think about how thankful you are for His love for you and His direction and guidance for your life. You can write your prayer below if you so desire.

_____

_____

_____

_____

_____

_____

_____

_____

_____

Week 4 Review & Meditation

WEEK 4
DAY 4

Today is your final weekly review! Congratulations for completing your journey through this aromatherapy Bible study and for finding out more about who you are and the vision God has put in your heart.

Step 1: Meditating on God's Word With Aromatherapy

Start today by making sure your diffuser is running with your chosen oil or by applying your oil in your preferred manner. Breathe it in deeply. Calm your mind. Reflect on the weekly scripture. Were you able to memorize it? How does it make you feel about the topic of vision in regard to your life? Are you ready to write down your vision?

> *"And the LORD answered me: 'Write the vision; make it plain on tablets, so he may run who reads it.'"*
> *Habakkuk 2:2 (ESV)*

Take time to read through the notes you have taken this week. Review your thoughts and prayers and see if you can write the scripture from memory. Write out as much as you can from memory here:

_____

_____

_____

_____

_____

Remember that 25 word statement you came up with? Write it in the box below:

Tomorrow, you will begin assembling your vision board. Do you have your materials? A framed corkboard is a nice option, but remember that there are many other options, such as poster board or plain paper. It's your board, so it's your choice.

You will be using the answers you have written in the boxes for each weekly review on your vision board. We suggest that you photocopy the pages and cut out the boxes, or type the answers from your boxes on a separate page to save you from cutting up your book.

Step 2: Journal and Pray

While diffusing and breathing in your oil blend, write out a prayer that engages the Father about how you feel about your vision. Commit your vision to Him and ask Him for help in seeing your vision fulfilled. He loves you so much. Philippians 1:6 tells us that God will be faithful to complete that which He starts in us. Commit your vision to Him and be expectant for this promise to be fulfilled.

Your Final Day
Assembling the Vision Board

WEEK 4
DAY 5

Habakkuk 2:2 (ESV)
"And the LORD answered me: 'Write the vision; make it plain on tablets, so he may run who reads it.'"

STEP 1: Meditating on God's Word With Aromatherapy

Diffuse your oil blend or apply it to your body and smell the fragrance purposefully for several minutes. Allow your mind to clear and go back through the four scriptures you have studied during this study, and read them out loud. Tell yourself that you want to remember these scriptures and make a mental note to associate the smell of this oil with these scriptures and the topic of vision for your life. When you are ready, move on to step 2.

STEP 2: Assemble Your Vision Board

Continue to diffuse your oil blend (or smell it purposefully from where you have applied it on your body) as you gather your materials and put it together.

Here are some steps to follow to help you complete your vision board:

- Photocopy all of the Weekly Review pages that have the boxes where you have written your vision statements. If you choose not to photocopy them, you may either cut these sections out of your book, or hand write or type your responses on a new sheet of paper.
- Cut out the boxes (or hand write the information) and tack or glue them to your corkboard.

Add any additional decoration that you like (or none at all). We've seen all kinds of things, such as a ribbon with a bow to hang the board, or a bow glued to the top and side. You can get as artsy (or not) as you choose! On the following pages you will find a few items for you to photocopy and use if you desire. You can create your own graphics if you are tech-savvy and enjoy that sort of thing.

Bring your finished board to your final Bible study meeting to share with the group. Then find a place to hang your board so that you see it every day. Congratulations for finishing!

Whenever your vision changes, or when you have something to add, just print it off or write it down and add it to your board. The vision can change, that is what is great about having a corkboard; you can add and remove things so that your vision always stays current.

Thank you for going through this study with us. We have more studies and resources available for you on our website, HolyScents.org. Please take a few minutes to visit our site and click on the "feedback" tab to let us know your thoughts about this book and study. We are grateful for the feedback, and we might even email you a thank-you surprise if you do! God bless you as you follow Him in the vision He has for your life!

-*Yvonne and Wendy*

My Vision Board

VISION BOARD

Where there is no vision the people perish.
Proverbs 29:18

Delight yourself also in the Lord, And He
shall give you the desires of your heart.
Commit your way to the Lord, Trust also
in Him, And He shall bring it to pass.
Psalm 37:4-5

For I know the plans I have for you, declares
the Lord, plans to prosper you and not to harm
you, plans to give you hope and a future.
Jeremiah 29:11

And the LORD answered me: "Write
the vision; make it plain on tablets,
so he may run who reads it."
Habakkuk 2:2

HolyScents.org

To obtain additional copies and for more information on other books by Growing Healthy Homes, please visit our website at www.GrowingHealthyHomes.com

The ABC's of Building a Young Living Organization

Conquering Toxic Emotions

Essentials: 50 Answers To Common Questions About Essential Oils

Gentle Babies

Road to Royal: Roadmap to Success